LONSDALE

RING CLASSICS

Fighting Was My Business

Other titles in the Lonsdale Ring Classics series:

Ten and Out! A Biography of Benny Lynch
Peter McInnes

Series editor: Peter McInnes

Fighting Was My Business

JIMMY WILDE

 Robson Books

Originally published in 1938. This Lonsdale Ring
Classics edition published in 1990 by Robson Books
Ltd, Bolsover House, 5–6 Clipstone Street, London
WIP 7EB

This Lonsdale Ring Classics edition copyright ©
Robson Books 1990

British Library Cataloguing in Publication Data

Wilde, Jimmy
  Fighting was my business. – 2nd ed – (Lonsdale
  ring classics.)
  1. Boxing – Biographies
  I. Title   II. Series
  796.830922

  ISBN 0 86051 642 3

Printed in Great Britain by
St Edmundsbury Press Ltd, Bury St Edmunds, Suffolk

CONTENTS

The Stud House,
Barley Thorpe,
Oakham

6th May 1938.

My dear Wilde,

      I hear you are writing a book and that you would like me to put a few lines of introduction to it. I should have thought you were so well known that no introduction was needed, but nothing gives me greater pleasure than to do as you wish, for I have known you over a great many years and apart from being an admirer of your science in pugilistic encounters, I also know you to be a very straightforward and honest man whose kindness and deeds are very much appreciated in your own district and for that reason alone I only hope the book will be a success, for I am sure it will be interesting to many and especially to all those who take an interest in boxing, in which you excelled.

Yours truly,
Lonsdale

FOREWORD

In the whole history of boxing there has never been anyone quite like Jimmy Wilde, known in his heyday by such *noms-de-guerre* as 'The Tylorstown Terror' and 'The Ghost with a Hammer in his Hand'. This minute Welshman was born on 15 May 1892 and, in his prime, stood no more than 5 feet 3 inches scaling well under seven stone.

Such a midget he was, so pale and apparently frail, that it almost defies belief that Wilde could have beaten the world, annihilating along the way scores of top-class men many pounds, and sometimes stones, heavier than himself. His first officially recorded contest was in 1910, the last coming in 1923 when Jimmy was deprived of the World 8-stone Championship after which he never donned a glove again.

But an incredible story lies not only between those landmarks but from the very earliest days of Wilde's life. Nat Fleischer's *Ring Record Books* record 153 fights beneath his name, but a far more likely estimate is the 800-plus which Jimmy told me he had recorded bout by bout from his very beginnings. It was in the later 1950s that I got to know the little Welshman. He then looked more like a portly, rubicund little Bishop and was coupling the duties of a doorman at the *News of the World* off Fleet Street with lending his name to a 'ghosted' boxing column in that journal.

It has to be realised that, even from school days, then the mines and the day he began taking on all-comers in a touring boxing booth, Wilde had knocked out boys and men bigger and more experienced than himself with almost ridiculous ease. He weighed less than a jockey, yet timing and leverage helped him punch harder than some heavyweights and with amazing accuracy and speed.

A fighter by instinct, the Welshman's style was unique to himself and he adapted his methods with wonderful cleverness to the needs of his size. To guard the blows of much bigger men would itself have taken its toll of Jimmy's strength so he guarded and blocked very little. Rather did he avoid by sheer speed, being just out of reach when an opponent tried to hit him. He explained this in a little instructional book called *The Art of Boxing* which was published under his name in a number of editions, but the truth is that his method would have been foolhardy to anyone other than Jimmy Wilde. For it stands to reason, does it not, that without quite exceptional speed plus intuition, an out-of-range fighter cannot counter-punch effectively. To an ordinary boxing mortal, the way to nullify punches is to come inside them and so minimise their effect.

Another important point to be borne in mind when viewing Wilde's amazing career in retrospect is that, during the years through which he was fighting professionally, the British Boxing Board of Control (1929) had not yet come into being. Had it been otherwise, that august body's Regulations would undoubtedly have restricted Jimmy's activities if only in the matters of conceding weight and the frequency of his ring battles.

During World War I my late father was Warrant Officer Class One in charge of the Display Team of what was then called the Army Gymnastic Staff, nowadays known as the Army Physical Training Corps. One of its boxing members was 'The Mighty Atom' (another affectionate soubriquet appended behind Wilde's name), other household names touring being those of Bombardier Billy Wells, Pat O'Keefe, Johnny Basham, Joe Beckett and fellow-Welshman Peerless Jim Driscoll.

My father knew his boxing and he always averred that Wilde was a natural and that his punching was sharp, precise and sustained rather than devastating through the force of any one particular blow. That he knew exactly where to strike and when to strike, and that because of the vast experience he had acquired in all sorts of rings nationwide relaxation rather than tension in action was the keynote of the whole Jimmy Wilde fighting operation.

In trying to describe boxing and boxers it is only too easy to compile what may appear to be complete contradictions. Because, for instance, while it is true that once Wilde had a man in trouble he would rain in punches non-stop and from all angles, on the other hand he rarely wasted a blow and his little knuckles were directed with almost compass-like precision.

The final word, before his own story re-unfolds again after these 52 years since it was first published, shall be that in 1959 Jimmy Wilde, 'The Mighty Atom', 'The Ghost with a Hammer in his Hand', 'The

Tylorstown Terror' – choose which you will – was entered in America's 'Boxing Hall of Fame' through *Ring Magazine*. That was thirty-six years after his final ring battle and the tribute surely speaks for itself. Had he been fighting in this day and age he would have made millions, the Wilde face would have been familiar to the entire populace through constant exposure on television and he would certainly have received a decoration.

CHAPTER I

★

ILL OMENS?

ONE OF THE EARLIEST THINGS I REMEMBER IS MY father reaching home from the pit, and washing vigorously at the bath tub. It was not only a ritual of cleanliness—up to a point—but it also coincided with meal time and in those days I was always ready to eat. Few of the children of the mining families in Tylorstown were over-nourished, and there were times, particularly during the strikes, when starvation was not far away.

But there is more to that daily washing ritual than its coincidence with food. I used to be sitting on the floor, or in a chair by the wall of the small living-room-and-kitchen that usually housed the whole family, when my father came in. He would be black-faced, in fact black everywhere, with the whites of his eyes and the red of his lips showing grotesquely vivid. Off would come his coat and shirt, and he would begin to splash and scrub face, arms, neck and chest. Then on would go a cleaner shirt kept for his " leisure " hours, and, according to what shift he was working, we would have breakfast or supper.

But once a week, usually on Fridays, there was a change in this ritual. With a great ado and help from my mother or my older sister *he would wash his back,* until that was as gleaming white as the rest of his body. The back was washed only that once in every seven days, and I learned afterwards that it was a general colliers' habit. That, of course, was before the days when baths were installed at the pit-heads so that a miner could be reasonably clean before reaching home. It was just one of the many difficulties that a housewife, with some pride in a frugal home, had to face.

I suppose my birthplace, Number 8 Station Road, Pontygwaith (Craig Berthllwyd, Quaker's Yard), next door to and really part of Tylorstown, was in no way different from the hundreds of other cottages lined up, all exactly alike to look at, all covered with the grime of the Rhondda Valley. And I suppose I was in no way different, in the early years, from the dozens of youngsters of my own age. As soon as we could stand up without the certainty of falling down after a couple of steps, we made the street our playground. We had our quarrels and repaired them, we formed in little cliques absurdly jealous of the privacy of our meetings and plans, and I suppose I was upwards of six before people began to single me out for trouble.

I swear I was not wholly to blame! I was hardly at fault because by some freak of nature I could keep standing longer than the other fellows, during a fight. And they were fights! No ropes and referees and anxious seconds, but a free-for-all, without any great concern for weight or knowledge of boxing rules. Probably one of the reasons why I escaped so lightly was the fact that I was so small. Even then I seemed stunted and under-nourished, a burden to my mother and at times an object of scorn to the other boys—

which latter, of course, caused most trouble. There was not enough of me to hit squarely and I proved an adept at dodging weighty blows and kicks, and getting in with a lot of quick punches that often caused pain, more often anger, and rarely did any damage.

This propensity for fighting at each and every opportunity soon got me into disgrace. There were gloomy forecasts about my future: I was a born trouble-maker, said the neighbours, with shaking heads. No good could come of a little morsel of flesh and bone that obstinately refused to take a good licking. (Or, from the Nonconformists, from a boy who always wanted to use his fists.)

Of course, in those days I was not conscious of any determination not to be knocked out. My chief thought was to enjoy myself, and I can safely say that I succeeded, despite the whippings and the scoldings and the threats that were reckoned to subdue me.

There was a great deal of talk about the " school knocking sense into me " later on. I grew up with a hatred of the idea of going to school and, mixing with boys who were already old pupils, I learned almost before I had started the many tricks of avoiding attendance. We would do a " mich," the colloquialism for playing truant, just as often as we dared —more often than good sense dictated—and my ill repute grew as rapidly at school as it had in Station Road. The grey heads shook again; I was reasoned with at length, threatened with violence—and often enough received it !—and generally subjected to all the diplomatic and strategic tricks of turning a young scallywag into a respectable and teacher-fearing scholar.

I don't think I deliberately wanted to cause trouble.
I just happened to get in the middle of it whenever
any was about. Consequently there were times when
I was accused of escapades of which I had no knowledge. Being blamed for these naturally filled me
with grievance, that futile, childish conviction of
adult injustice, but that again had no lasting effect.
Despite a great deal of prejudice and dislike my early
days, even at school, were happy. There were highlights, of course !

One of the red-letter days of my first seven years
was when—during a " mich "—I met a little party
of elder boys walking into the street, all carrying
bulging sacks on their shoulders. Puzzled, I persuaded my sister—Mary Anne was just over a year
older than I and we had a great deal in common—
that the spectacle was worth investigating. The
sacks were deposited behind an old shed, where no
one was likely to look for them. Mary Anne and
I waited until the party was safely out of sight before
making a furtive visit to the hiding place.

" What will it be ? " Mary Anne asked in a whispe..

" It will be rabbits or birds, they'll have been
poaching," I said confidently, and with high hopes of
an unusually succulent meal.

But the contents were harder than any rabbit or
partridge, and we opened the neck of a sack quickly.

" Why, and it is coal ! " Mary Anne said with
genuine surprise, and we stared at the little shining
lumps of coal in mingled disappointment and curiosity.
It afforded a great deal of conversation for us that
day—we shared many secrets—and we formed a plan
that was simple enough to carry out. The party we

had seen, consisting of three boys, was often late at school, and as often out in the evenings. Moreover, they had more money than the average coal-miner's sons.

I was up early the next morning, watching the path they had taken on the previous day. It was raining a fine drizzle and I had no reward for the tiresome vigilance, while the trio reached school on time. This happened three times in succession, until I began to despair, but just before five on the fourth morning I saw my quarry. Dawn was breaking as they made their way boldly along the path.

I went back quickly for Mary Anne and we hurried in their wake. We had an idea where they were going after the first half mile. To the tips!

The tips, where the coal was stacked, were some four miles from the house, and it was not difficult to collect a sack of small lumps. Mary Anne and I fell over ourselves to find some sacks, and followed the trio's example. Our venture passed off successfully, and no one saw us. But those sacks weighed all of three-quarters of a hundred-weight, and we were in a state of collapse when we eventually reached Tylerstown.

We hid our hauls before going on to school, each to get a caning and detention for the evening. But the trio suffered the same fate and we had time to find their next move. Following them at a discreet distance after school we saw them collect their sacks and carry them to streets some distance away. Here the coal seemed to fetch a good reward. Mary Anne, who at times had more courage than I, inquired about the price. Sometimes a shilling was paid, and nine-pence was a safe bet! We earned one-and-ninepence on our first deal and thereafter decided to make it a daily habit.

Alas ! The gathering of coal was a regular practice, and we had merely forestalled our mother's orders to get it, and thus help in the family budget. There were to be no rosy dreams of wealth.

It seemed to us, however, that the nearer tips would afford just as easy access, and we would have nothing like so far to carry the coal. One morning's venture went off all right, and we were actually early for school !

On the second morning we had our sacks half full when I caught sight of a pair of boots moving stealthily on the other side of a truck. With a shout of warning, I swung the sack over my shoulder and ran for all I was worth, with Mary Anne no more than a couple of yards behind. Thanks to the rails over which our pursuer fortuitously stumbled we managed to escape. But we had had a scare ; we knew that we would get into serious trouble if we were caught ; even recognition had its dangers.

" That will be why the others go so far," Mary Anne said that evening. " Even should they be seen no one will know them. We'll go as far, Jimmy, that we will."

From then on we never raided a pit-head nearer than five miles from our own little village, and for a long time we carried out our raids successfully. At some tips we knew there was danger, but most of the men on duty were prepared to let us take coal once a week. Consequently we kept away from a pit-head for five or six days after a visit. Now and again when an inspector or other official was near we

would have a race for our safety, leaving a trail of
coal behind us. But even then the regular watchers
would often warn us. One old fellow, who walked
with a bad limp as a result of a mine accident, would
cock his head on one side, half-close his right eye
and leave the other wide open and say :

" There'll be trouble for those that come this
morning, my young people. Trouble, trouble ! "

We knew better than to ignore the warning and
off we would go for safer fields. It was rare that we
returned home empty handed.

After nearly a year a stricter watch was kept on
the pit-heads to prevent pilfering. The oldest exponents of the art were scared off when some three
or four were caught and taken by the police. Mary
Anne and I were thankful for our escape, and it was
decided to suspend our activities until safer times.

It was my mother who first started us black-
berrying. Sometimes men or women would come
round with barrows of the fruit, selling it very cheaply,
and yet dear enough for the slender Tylorstown
pockets. Children from nearby houses would pick a
few bushels of berries from the stunted bushes close at
hand, but Mary Anne and I decided to go further afield.

Not until we had many futile walks did we find
a really good place for the berries. It was in the
mountains, some seven miles away from home. But
up we would get before dawn and trapes over the
hills, to come back with as many as a dozen bushels
of ripe blackberries, selling those that were not
needed at home and completely free from danger.
Shame that it was only a seasonal trade ! Whinberries
came in useful, too.

I sometimes wonder whether it was a simple desire to earn money that sent me cheerfully on those long walks and procured me beatings and—yes, kickings—from the masters for being late : or, at least, for being late and also cheeky when reprimanded. When upbraided I could never find the sense not to smile ! It might have been that inbred money-consciousness of the mining districts, or just a longing to do something other than standing about and quarrelling with the rest of the boys.

Unfortunately even these extra activities did not keep me from fighting. Our cliques were as solid and antagonistic to others as ever, but as the years passed the fighting grew a little more organised.

Not one of us did not have a boxing hero. So many boxers came from the nearby villages, fighting usually at the boxing booths, that most of us knew one or two names that were mentioned occasionally in the papers. The height of fame ! Every district, too, boasted its mountain fighters, grand old fellows who fought, bare-fisted and naked to the waist, to a standstill. Gory sights many of them were, caked with blood and sweat on face and body.

I would spend my precious pennies and get as close to the ring as I could, goggling at the clumsy fighting, inspired by the spell of the ring. How I loved its tawdry magnificence ! How I envied the challengers, who dared step in the ring, only to get slaughtered. How often I imagined doing the same thing one day, but with a difference. I could never picture myself being laid out as easily as many of the unfortunate combatants who were prepared to be knocked out a hundred times for a one-in-a-thousand chance of earning a pound for lasting a round.

Probably it did me little good to feel that I was invincible, but experiences in the streets and during the free fights at least gave me an excuse. I was abnormally small, of course, but now no one seemed inclined to taunt me about that. I can remember fighting, being knocked down, recovering, going down again, until I hardly knew how to get to my feet. Yet somehow or other I was always standing when the other fellow gave it up, or the police came and sent us scuttling away. You always had to have the strength left for the run from the law!

I read avidly everything that I could about boxing, and anyone who had ever appeared in the ring seemed to me a demi-god, although I was hardly familiar with that term. This was before I was ten, when I was supposed to have no formed idea of my own.

In any case, I was booked for the mines.

I know my parents were longing for the day when I would be earning regularly. As in many mining homes, there was little parental affection spared, although perhaps I should say there was little shown. Each child was an expense, another mouth to feed, until twelve or thirteen years passed. Then off to the mines as a boy, to learn the craft of cutting coal, to suffer the first horrors of going down the pit and gradually to become just another miner, burrowing like a rabbit out of the light of the sun.

There was no other way of earning a livelihood, and in those early days—I am talking of the time when I was nine and ten—boxing never appeared to be more than a spare-time occupation for anyone.

I knew no full-time professionals and only vaguely realised their existence.

Even at school boxing became spare-time.

I knew, of course, that a boxer who smoked was asking for bad wind, and failure. But I was also surrounded by a hundred or so boys, some younger than myself, who would smoke at the least opportunity. Many of us collected the fag-ends thrown away at home—how often we would revolt when the elders threw the ends in the fire!—and not to smoke was to admit oneself to be something subnormal. (In parenthesis I might say that I have not smoked since I was sixteen, and have never touched alcohol apart from a single glass of champagne after my big fights.)

Then someone started offering " prize-money " for fighting. A penny packet of cigarettes was the prize, and the fights had to last until one or the other of the combatants was completely out of action.

We would go to a lot of trouble with these fights. A rough ring would be formed, seconds were appointed with dignity, although no one seemed anxious for the task of refereeing. There were side-bets to every fight and fairness was usually ensured because of the anger of the crowd after a foul blow.

At first my size was an obstacle. The fights were usually between the older and bigger boys. But I persisted in getting a " match " and, one dull day, stood opposite a youth three stone heavier than myself. I often think back on that day with amusement : I had no idea how often I was going to give a stone and more away in the ring.

I know that I had no hearty backers. Most of the crowd were convinced I had no earthly chance. It's queer, but I was *sure* of winning. I don't think it was bravado; I'm sure it was not bumptiousness, for it was impossible to get high-and-mighty in that environment. In fact I told no one of my confidence. I just weighed into my opponent.

Details are blurred now. I remember the surprise on his face when I stung him with sharp blows and then darted out of range. I can remember his curses because I was never close enough to be hit by his heavy, swinging blows. And I remember at last we stood face to face and slogged away. There was a stupefied silence when at last it was over, and I was rocking on my pins. But the favourite was a lump on the muddy ground, unable to rise.

No cigarettes had ever tasted so sweet as that " prize-money " !

None the less smoking worried my conscience: no " boxer " took risks with his wind ! But cigarettes were the prize and after winning them they had to be smoked. I would get several packets some weeks and my " seconds " usually shared the fruits of victory. The fights attracted a lot of attention at the school and elsewhere; few believed that my four stone could get the better of seven-, eight- and nine-stone fighters who had quite a lot of bare-knuckle experience.

With my increased proficiency at fighting, my notoriety grew. My adventures were generally acknowledged to be a bad omen for the future, and I think my mother and father lived in fear of my getting into serious trouble. But nature had been kind to me in one way. It had not given me height and weight, but it had given me the queer, wiry strength that had always stood me in such good stead, and it had presented me with a cheerful outlook on life. I laughed a lot at things. There were times when I enraged masters and other elders by a smile, doubtless called an impudent grin, but I think it helped to convince them that only sheer animal spirits kept me in mischief—nothing vicious. At least, I hope it convinced them!

There are, of course, several landmarks standing out in my early schooldays. The start of the coal trips was one of them and that habit lasted on and off until I left school. The first " big " fight was another. And one of the most important was one for which I received no opprobrium, a rare thing for me in those days.

The first rumours of the trouble were well ahead of the actual facts. But even at that age, for I could have been no more than eight, I knew the meaning of the dreaded word " strike." I knew what hunger and misery it could bring. I heard women talking of it in tones of horror and dismay. Yet strikes there had always been; they were as inevitable as life itself.

I do not remember the rights or wrongs of the trouble, but I do know the belief in the coming of a big strike increased. And then, when it started, it was not in the mines.

The railways, so vital to coal-mining, lost their patience first, and the great strike of 1911 started. Gradually it had its stifling effect on the mines. My father and brothers were put off, and although there was a certain amount of relief money available, it was not enough to keep us in food: hunger began to make itself felt acutely.

I had to earn money.

There was no chance then of getting it from sacks of coal : no one had the money to buy the fuel, even if the watch at the pits was relaxed enough to allow me—and others—to pilfer it. But wherever a big body of the strikers was centred there was a certain amount of money available.

And the weather grew hot.

I cannot claim to be the inventor of the idea (our parents were) but I can say that Mary Anne and I were among the first to take it up. We made small beer, a mixture of herbs including dandelions, with balm, or the froth from beer, to serve as yeast; and then, after taking it for miles over the rough country, we sold it to the strikers. Before and after school we were busy, and there was always someone ready to " mich " so as to look after the sales during the day. It was not as profitable as the coal and black-berries had been during the better times, but at least it was a way of getting a little extra money for food, while the strikers welcomed us. In a way it was perhaps the most unforgettable period of my schooldays.

Unless the final labour examination takes pride of place when I was due to qualify for a " pass-out " into the adult world of the mines.

It was necessary to get the certificate, but it was almost impossible to fail. I hated the idea, despite a certain hankering to earn a grown-up's money, which I fondly imagined would be the reward. But as it was inevitable I took it with as good a grace as I could.

There was one great thing to lure me on. I knew

there were a number of old boxers and even real mountain fighters at the pits, and I might be lucky enough to get in touch with some of them. At that time, when I was between twelve and thirteen, I would listen wide-eyed to any stories of the ring, while one of the idols of my youth was getting into prominence, namely Freddie Welsh, later the light-weight champion of the world and himself a local product.

So I passed the examination, and prepared for the mines. There was to be no holiday. One day school, the next day the pit-head and the dreaded cage. I remember my father was in bad health at the time, and my mother was not often indoors. The atmo-sphere at home was strained, uncomfortable. With this, and the realisation that there would be no more " miching," no more fights for cigarettes with school-mates, I think I approached the first day with fear and trembling.

The heavy boots hurt my feet as I tramped to the office, and was duly enrolled. The clerk glanced at my tiny form, and laughed, making comments that fired me with indignation, and a desire to prove I could do what any of the others could do. I joined the band with whom I was to travel down the cage, and in my anger I forgot my fears and regrets. Nor did I dream that I was soon to meet the man who was to become my father-in-law, and what undoubtedly would have seemed more important at the time, the man who was one of the stalwarts of the renowned mountain fighters. He was to teach me the rudi-ments of boxing, the only early training that I had, and to second me in the ring times out of number.

CHAPTER II

★

TWO BOB A DAY

IT IS NOT EASY FOR ME TO REMEMBER MY OWN FEELINGS during that first spell of work. I suppose they were vague, and I hardly knew my own wishes, although the ambition of fighting for fighting's sake was always very strong in me. I do not think I ever seriously expected to be able to get away from the mines, and to become a professional boxer. Such an ambition seemed far beyond my range, particularly because of my insignificant size. I weighed little more than four stone and stood about four feet six, a positive bag of bones, but a bag that had never been punctured. I do not remember a day's illness in my life, apart from early childhood complaints.

Then for some months all ambition and hope was knocked out of me.

There has been a great deal written about the horrors of the first trip down the pit-shaft. It was, in a way, terrifying, but most of what I have read about it is exaggerated unless I was less sensitive than the average beginner, and I have good reason to doubt that.

I knew most of the men in the shift well, of course, but that did little to cheer me. I was wearing cut-down clothes that had already seen pit-life, and they seemed absurdly big about me. There were some forty of us in the shift, and I remember the call of " Hold tight ! ", the gate closing, and then the descent, which seemed slow at first, and then bewilderingly fast. Daylight disappeared like a quick dusk. Soon the blackness was only broken by a few of the safety lamps which seemed to spread no effective light. Then my stomach seemed to want to leave me. I seemed to go upwards, not down, and I expected to see daylight any moment. The breath had been knocked out of me, an inevitable feeling at the first descent, although one that soon disappeared. Yet it took a surprisingly short time to descend the thousand-odd feet of the mine.

My first impressions were of water, deafness and darkness. When I did start to hear, a whisper seemed like a shout, particularly my own. The others were used to talking in a cadence that just fitted in with the mine. One of the owners gripped my shoulder in friendly fashion, and told me to stand aside for a few minutes, and watch. Gradually I was able to see things more clearly. The rails for the trams, the safety lamps shining on the wet, slimy walls, and the road, where it was difficult to keep a footing, and reflecting on the water oozing out everywhere. I remember the great battens and staves that held the roof up, but my biggest memory was the fright I had when I heard a rolling along the rails towards me.

I did not think what it was, and from the roaring din I imagined there was a fall, the dreadful word that spelt untold misery up on the surface. I held myself tense, hardly daring to move.

" Come on, young 'un," said my kindly mentor,

and he half pulled me into a manhole, just before the trams passed and I was too scared to ask what the noise had been. But further along the road I saw the trams often enough and soon understood.

I thanked my stars that I had not asked questions. There was a bluff heartiness about the miners, little sympathy was wasted on youngsters down for the first time, but all the same there was a genuine kindliness. I felt that I was among friends : I needed that feeling !

It is now over thirty years since I started work at the wage of two shillings a day. That seemed a fortune, although apart from a few coppers it would all go into the home. Many of the duties have grown vague. None of them was exciting, if some, because of the general atmosphere of the mine, were a little frightening.

For some time my size worked against me—or for me, it is hard to say which—even down the mine. I looked too fragile to tackle the heavier work. Most of my time was spent in watering the coal dust, watching the ponies and checking the trucks as they came through. It was not exacting work, except the truck-watching. They had to be counted, and passed as full, each truck containing a ton or more of fresh-hewn coal. But despite the lack of heavy work at first, I found I grew terribly tired. At the end of a shift I was ready for food and sleep, and nothing else. Sleep was in fact more like a coma.

My boxing ambitions were not consciously set back. I just did not possess the mental energy to think about anything. It was a kind of dull, vague nightmare.

There were always accidents. Rarely did a day pass

without some mishap or other. None of them was serious, and I was lucky never to be in a big explosion. But there would be falls, crushing a man's limbs so that he would never work again. " Minor " accidents where there was so much blood that I was horrified, and sick. But the others took it all for granted and the injured men seemed to think nothing of it. Although in considerable pain, they would laugh and joke about their own carelessness. I had a growing feeling that the miners, instead of being the callous, crude men they seemed above the earth, were a race apart, possessing a courage that seemed unnatural.

At first then I hated the work, but like the rest I grew accustomed to it. There was little or no relief from the monotony, but gradually I understood the rough jokes, the constant stories that circulated. And, as there will be wherever Welsh miners meet, talk of boxing. Slowly my interest and hopes in the sport were revived.

Then I discovered that Dai Davies, one of the oldest mountain fighters in Wales, was in the pit.

The mountain fighters, who exist to this day, although the bouts are more secret now than they were in those days, were a class apart. They were descendants, in a boxing sense, from the bare-knuckle days of the Regency. Fantastic tales of the strength of the combatants reached me. There was talk of men lasting thirty and forty rounds, and being as fresh at the end of it as at the beginning. I learned soon that it was no exaggeration. What made it more remarkable was that the fighters would finish a heavy shift, have a two or three hours' sleep, and then *walk* as many as ten or twelve miles across the mountains to a fight lasting for hours. The mountain tracks were very different from what they are now. Few roads had been made, and the walking was rough, over rocks and gravel, sometimes with long ascents with gradients of one in five or six.

Often the champions came from villages twenty and thirty miles apart and the crowds came even further afield, for each widespread district had its champion.

It was an organised sport, although opposed by the authorities, and conducted with " secrecy." The police, of course, knew about the contests, but turned a blind eye. When all was said and done, some of the venues were so inaccessible that it would have needed a platoon of soldiers to have reached the spot, and to break up the crowds.

These forty- and fifty-round battles, with bare knuckles, were quite the order of the day. Each round lasted as long as both men kept on their feet. There was, of course, a referee and seconds. Everything was kept in strict order, although the rules were different from those of the canvas ring.

I remember seeing Dai Davies one day, with his face battered and the knuckles of his hands raw. This was when he had me working with him as his assistant—or " boy." He smiled easily when I asked him what he had been doing.

" Just keeping fit, boy, just keeping fit."

But by then I was aware that Dai, under a cover of roughness and threats at what he would do to inquisitive boys, was kindly and friendly. I persisted.

" Well, if you must know, I was fighting," he admitted, his blue eyes twinkling.

" How long did it last ? " I was agog with

curiosity and ready at once to look on Dai as a hero deserving worship.

" Oh, thirty-nine rounds," he said, " and I will admit I wasn't sorry my man did not feel like any more. Was it hot in the hills ! "

Thirty-nine rounds with bare fists, knuckles raw and face battered almost out of recognition. All for a few pounds !

But instead of being appalled, it revived all my own desires. But I was wise enough at the time to keep the ideas to myself. Dai was a big man, and I learned a lot about him afterwards. His wife was a strict chapel-goer, and strongly disapproved of fighting. Some idea of Dai's nature can be gathered from the fact that he continued to fight and retained his wife's affection. He had a daughter, a year or two younger than myself, who—but that is anticipating.

It seemed madness to think of my puny four-and-a-half stone engaged with the hardy old mountain fighters, and I nursed a conviction that I would grow tall suddenly. The older folk were often saying that between fourteen and fifteen I would shoot up. But I obstinately refused to gain much in inches or weight. It was not lack of food, for I had enough ; as much if not more than any of the other miners, and often more than my father. He was still ailing, and found the work at the pit more than he could stand. There was a growing tension between him and my mother and I knew that they were not happy. Looking back, it is hard to blame either of them. Only the physically fit were really pulling their weight in the home or down the pit, terms which were actually synonymous. And father was a long way from fit.

At the time, of course, I thought little of it.

Now I was working at the coal-face. The work there, calling for crouching and often lying on the stomach to get at the seam, showed me to one advantage. Being small, I could easily get in low stalls where the bigger man found it hard. I would sometimes be able to start a seam, thus letting Dai work harder and getting the tram raced more quickly. To race a tram meant to fill it, putting a wall of big lumps of coal round the side and making a " wall " ; the smaller stuff went inside, so that it would not fall off. No matter how hard the seam, nor what difficulties in the way, six of those trams had to be filled by two men—or a man and a boy—before they earned a full week's wage. And that wage was barely enough to keep body and soul together.

I was in my element with Dai.

Not only was I proving useful, and more than pulling my weight, but as the picks swung Dai would tell me stories of the mountain fights. Some of the legendary stories were almost incredible. There were times when I could not believe them, but I know now they were true without exception. Dai would no more lie than he would strike his wife.

Occasionally Dai would break off, lay down his pick and, crouching in the gloom, with his face covered with coal dust and his hands and body black, demonstrate this punch or that. I grew to recognise semi-technical terms more readily. The upper-cut, the straight left, the essentials of defence : virtually all he knew.

It was typical of his modesty that someone else should first tell me of the historic fight he had with

Ted Chops (Williams) in the mountains behind the valley.

The two veterans of fighting had stood face to face and slogged at each other for eighty-four rounds ! The fight had lasted several hours, at the end of which Dai had won on a knock-out.

I taxed Dai with this.

" That is so," he answered with the slow, easy smile I was learning to appreciate so much. " Yes, it was a fine fight that, and Ted Chops was a grand fighter ! Tell me, Jimmy, is it true ye have ideas about serious fighting yourself ? "

I coloured furiously, but as I was hacking at a seam, and covered with dust, no one could see that.

" It is so, Dai, but with my weight what can I do ? "

" I've heard stories," said Dai, slipping in a word when the noise lessened a little. A sentence would sometimes last for three or four minutes, and a brief conversation, such as I am relating, be spread over an hour, for we dared not slack. " You seem to stand up well to those above your weight."

" It's nothing," I said. " They think they can finish me in no time, and I'm too fast for them."

" That's true," said Dai. " Your feet are as important as your hands, Jimmy, as I've told you often enough. One day I'll see you fight. We might be able to make something of you."

" You really think I could ? " I asked incredulously.

" Didn't your hero, Freddie Welsh, begin in much the same way ? " asked Dai. " And is he much bigger or heavier than you ? "

To be compared with Freddie Welsh, even in that vague fashion, gave me a joy that I had not experienced before. Dreams began to take a clearer shape. If Welsh had succeeded, against the obstacles of weight, height and the mines, why shouldn't I? I longed for the day to come when I would be able to show Dai what I could do, and a bond of friendship was forged between us.

I listened to his advice, his teaching down there in the depths, points of tactics that sometimes took an hour to explain in short, hurried sentences. And, as I was growing more used to the life, I would practise the stances and blows he talked of, when I was off shift. Usually we went to his home and, because of Mrs. Davies' objections, " fought " in the tiny bedroom! I went to the house also, when selling the sand that was put on the doorsteps, and grew to know his daughter well by sight, although we spoke very little.

Those bedroom bouts are perhaps worthy of more explanation. The room, like all those in the Tylorstown cottages, was tiny, and even with the bed pushed against the wall and the other furniture placed on top of it, there was all too little space. But Dai pointed out the less space to move in, the more important was quick footwork and bodywork. That showed me how a move of an inch or even less could make all the difference to the power of a blow given or received. Still further caution had to be exercised, for Dai did not want to make noise enough to disturb his wife. Yet at the end of an hour we would be dog-tired.

There were not many fights available in those days, for time was limited. But now and again I would get an opportunity at a street-end, where there was no fear of interference. I was never able to get a match with anyone my own weight, of course. Three and four stones was nothing to give away. And there, just as it has always been, I did not think seriously of the possibility of losing.

The fights were usually arranged some days beforehand, and as often as not I had seen my opponents in action. I had seen, too, that all of them had different styles of fighting. And I knew that I had to find their weaknesses, particularly against a small opponent.

Some of those fights lasted for ever, or so it seemed. I would get a battering that should have sent me to sleep a dozen times. Whether it was will-power, sheer physical strength, unsuspected even then, or just good luck I don't know. I do know that I was always standing at the end of a fight.

Dai heard the reports from time to time.

He was living at Tylorstown, but apart from the week-end fighting, when he was always in the mountains, he found his home interests allowed him little or no time to spare for me, outside those bedroom spars.

He saw me in action at last, however, when another boy in the mine annoyed me (or I annoyed him) and we settled a heated argument by taking our coats off, and fighting in a ring of enthusiastic miners. Fights were by no means uncommon down there, of course.

My opponent was Tommy Davies, a thick-set youngster with some booth fighting experience who, at nine stone, was three stone heavier than me.

For several rounds I danced away from him, although he landed several hearty punches, but I managed to stop him getting a follow up and a " kill." He rapidly grew angry and, being angry, grew careless.

I was not to know that it was the most important thing that had ever happened to me. Its result was not immediately obvious, and for some time afterwards I used the same method without realising properly what I was doing, or why I did it.

Tommy came out from his corner once with a " now I'll show you " expression, and his arms going like flails. It was the crudest fighting ever, but with his extra weight he should have overwhelmed me. He obviously intended to stop me dancing away. To his surprise, and the surprise of the spectators, I fell in with his plans. I stopped where I was, feet planted a foot and a half apart, tucked my chin in, and as he came with his defence wide open I let fly with all I knew with my right fist.

It connected.

Tommy was moving fast towards me, and my punch took him on the point. I remember a shock running through my body, and yet nothing was so startling as to see Tommy staggering backwards, to collapse and to stay on the ground while he was counted out.

But as I say, I did not realise what a lesson I had taught myself in ring-craft.

Dai was pleased without being enthusiastic and he decided to introduce me to the booths. And——

At fifteen I did not think much about girls. But with Mrs. Davies always ready with a cup of tea after the unsuspected demonstration I could not fail to get better known to 'Lisbeth. She was thirteen at the time, and a dressmaker, work that was something above my level. We still spoke very little to each other, and I sometimes wondered why she seemed

so morose. I learned soon afterwards, when I had
taken up lodgings with Dai.

Dai took a beating in the mountains. He was
getting old for fighting and he arrived home more
battered than ever. I was there, waiting to hear the
result of the fight. 'Lisbeth was with me.

At the sight of her father her expression was
stormy.

" 'Tis madness ! " she called out, to my astonish-
ment. " Fight, fight, fight, you'll one day be getting
yourself killed ! "

I gaped.

" But—but surely you *like* to think he's a
champion ? "

" Champion nothing ! " cried 'Lisbeth. " It will
be the ruin of him and any that fights with him. You
as well, Jimmy Wilde, it will be the ruin of you.
I hate fighting ! "

If anything had been wanted to discourage romantic
notions about 'Lisbeth that was it. I lived for fighting, and it seemed incredible that anyone young could
dislike the fame of the ring. Older folk, like Mrs.
Davies, were excused, of course. But 'Lisbeth was
adamant. Sometimes we took to strolling out
together, but she quickly tired of my efforts to persuade her that fighting was a manful occupation.
The time came when she would deliberately avoid
me. I was amused, and at the time made no great
efforts to force my attentions on her.

It was soon after this that I had one of the biggest
disappointments of my life. It also nearly ruined
any hopes I had of a boxing career.

The days at the coal-face were always brightened

by Dai's company. I looked forward to it, and I think he did. There were times when I was given other work than hewing and I detested being away from him. But the blow fell when I was shifted to work at the pit-head.

It was better paying than before, and I should have been pleased, but I hated it. None the less, the oracle or the manager had spoken. I spent my shifts above the ground, checking the trams as they were rolled from the pit-head to the sidings, and oiling the pulleys. There were times when I could sit in the sunshine, with little to do, and brood. At others I had more than enough work to occupy myself.

The accident happened, as accidents will, suddenly, and without any warning. I was alone, oiling the sheaves of the pulleys which were in almost constant motion, pulling thick steel ropes at speed and hauling the journey of trams—ten in all—loaded with coal over nearly two miles of uneven country. The rope swung as I was working, knocking me off my feet. Before I knew what had happened I was lying on the ground with the fast-moving rope going over me. I laid horrified, too frightened at first to shout.

When the journey stopped, some mile away from where I was lying, I managed to crawl away.

I was conscious of a pain in my right leg, but hardly knew what it was. I turned my head cautiously, and the sight of the blood that had soaked the trouser-leg and was spilling over the ground almost made me faint. A deep hole had been carved in the back of the calf, nearer the ankle than the knee.

To this day I don't know how I crawled away from that terrifying rope. There were little manholes along the track, at intervals of every twenty or thirty yards, and I knew if I could reach one of them, the pulley would no longer touch me. I shouted as I crawled, but no one heard me. And with each movement more damage was done to my leg.

Half-fainting, sick with loss of blood, I at last dropped into a hole. There I laid for over an hour and I do not remember being found and lifted out. But I do remember the bluff, kindly face of Dr. Morris, the pit doctor.

" Now, my boy, what have you been up to? We'll soon have you right ! "

I don't think I believed him even then.

I know that it was agony to have the wound dressed. The flesh had been torn away from the bone, coal-dust and dirt had done their work. In a day or two proud flesh developed. There was talk of amputation, a horror that almost made me faint.

I implored Dr. Morris to save the leg.

" I'll try," he always promised. " Don't worry, Jimmy, you'll be all right. I'll do all I can."

No man could have kept his word better. He dressed the wound regularly, made me as comfortable as I could be and, eventually, said that he could save the leg.

" But it will mean crutches for a month or two, Jimmy."

Well, crutches for a couple of months were better than a leg and a half for ever. Of course, on my sick-pay I was not able to pay my way, but I found friends and relatives wonderfully helpful. There can be no better place than mining villages for a man in trouble.

With a great deal of time on my hands, I read every available thing on boxing. Thumb-marked and torn books, old newspapers, everything that came my way. When time came that I could hobble far enough I would go to the library and read the current boxing news. It was almost worth being off work!

Freddie Welsh was rapidly forging ahead at this time, and I longed to emulate him. But would my leg really heal so that I stood a chance?

He occasionally gave exhibition bouts at local halls and I managed to watch him occasionally. I was staggered by his speed in the ring, and my hopes dwindled Could anyone be as swift and hard-hitting? Freddie, of course, was a fine boxer, if not as perfect as I thought at the time.

Meanwhile "two or three months" lengthened. I grew to forget what it was like to be without a crutch. I found Dai Davies very friendly, and naturally I saw quite a lot of 'Lisbeth. At least she could not blame this accident on boxing!

I sometimes wonder whether I was brooding over fighting when the accident happened, but that hardly seemed a wise thing to say to her.

Dr. Morris was reassuring, despite the length of my infirmity. If I would be patient and keep to the crutch, he would have me as good as ever. And he was true to his word, although the scar of the wound was ugly. To this day it remains—a blue mark, nearly two inches in diameter, and the flesh has never grown properly again. But I have had no great pain with it, and it has never let me down when I have been in the ring. None the less I have been told that

no one with a wound like that ought to be able to
stand up in the ring !

It was soon afterwards that I started boxing-booth
fighting.   Jack Scarrott's booth was often near
Tylorstown, and a shilling or two could be earned.
I was more intrigued at the time by the chance of
putting on fighting kit—with real gloves !—and getting some experience of the ring.   The long " holiday " had confirmed one thing.   I was going to get
away from the pit, and I was going to earn a living
by boxing.

I always earned my pay after becoming one of
Scarrott's string of boxers, but I had a shock one
evening.

'Lisbeth, of course, had no idea of the bedroom
tuition in the house, and I had by this time worried
the life out of her.   I would follow her frequently,
despite a lack of encouragement, and the dislike of
her friends.   Although a miner, Dai Davies was comparatively well-to-do, and his wife's friends, which
meant his daughter's circle, were rather above my head.

Imagine my jitters when, lined up for my turn at
the ring, I saw 'Lisbeth sitting in the booth, with
a girl friend !   I went perilously near to losing the
bout, but I had a reward of sorts, for I dressed
hurriedly and managed to catch 'Lisbeth up.   After
some discussion I had a kind of negative permission
to see her home.

" So you're interested in boxing," I said hopefully.
" And I thought——"

" It was —— who persuaded me," snapped 'Lisbeth, " and I think it's the most degrading thing I've
ever seen !   I hate it ! "

I had a suspicion that she wanted to say that she hated me, too, but the sentence was never uttered, although I fancy at the time it was near the truth. However, the cat was out of the bag with a vengeance, and my chances of marriage with 'Lisbeth seemed negligible. Even the winning of a handsome coffee set, supposedly of real silver, did not convince her of boxing's attractiveness—that same coffee set melted on the mantelpiece when fires started !

It was soon afterwards that I plucked up courage to ask 'Lisbeth to marry me. My persistence, mind you, had made it obvious that the plea was coming sooner or later, but for once I went into battle without the conviction that I would win. Certainly I was not prepared for her answer.

" And if I do, will you give up boxing ? "

I just stared. There, in a flash, was a choice between the two things that had come to matter more than anything else in my life. To marry 'Lisbeth, or to box.

" And—and if I do, will you marry me ? "

" Jimmy—please ! "

And so I capitulated. Some months afterwards, on a miner's wage of three pounds ten shillings a fortnight, we were married. I borrowed a suit from a friend for the occasion ! We found our own cottage and for a month or two I kept away from the booths. But it was becoming increasingly obvious that I could not give up fighting for ever. And I was slowly beginning to realise that by working diplomatically I could get back to the ring—such as it was—and keep peace at home.

CHAPTER III

★

CHOCOLATE ALMONDS AND BOOTH DAYS

APART FROM HER DISLIKE OF BOXING, INSTILLED chiefly by her mother, 'Lisbeth had one weakness: for chocolate almonds.

On our thirty-five shillings a week there was little enough to spare for any kind of luxury. I had long since given up smoking, even though I still occasionally won a box of cigarettes in a fight. To look after my " entertainment expenses " I had sixpence a week. Chocolate almonds have never been the cheapest of sweets, and it can hardly be wondered at that ' Lisbeth on being presented with a quarter of a pound most Saturdays, began to wonder how I managed to get them. I confess inventing all manner of weird explanations, but I soon suspected that she was beginning to guess the truth.

I was fighting, of course, when I was not on shift down the mine.

Scarrott's booth was still in full swing, but when it was close home the neighbours talked. I went further afield, and gained a wider experience. I used to be annoyed at the laughter that would go up when my skinny frame was inserted between the ropes, but it was not long before I grew used to the silence of surprise after I had pulled off another knock-out, and the roar of applause that came afterwards. The annoyance quickly faded.

'Lisbeth's did not, when at last she asked me outright whether I was boxing.

I had no objection to keeping up the deception provided there was no direct lie involved, but this was a different matter. I think my school-masters would have recognised my smile as I nodded. Few people will believe that I never feel nervous without grinning like a half-wit.

" It's doing no harm, and it's helping me to save," I said.

" It's helping to be your ruin ! " I could see that 'Lisbeth was really upset. Yet, chiefly because of my continual wins, which were beginning to make me feel that I *had* something different from the average fighter, and Dai's constant encouragement, I realised that I had to stand out now. As a matter of fact, it was our first serious difference, made worse by the fact that a child was on the way.

" If trouble comes," I said, without the need for saying a " strike," " the money will be precious useful. And I don't get hurt ; no one ever marks me."

That was true. I was lucky to be practically unmarked after the fights, which had made 'Lisbeth uncertain for so long about the source of the chocolate almonds. But although I had broken the promise made before marriage I would not make it again. 'Lisbeth hated the fighting, I know, but there it was. Boxing was stronger than anything else in me. But I began to be afraid it would cause real unhappiness between us. At the time—about six months after our marriage—'Lisbeth was just past sixteen, I was not quite eighteen. We were hardly old enough to be stable in our ideas, or our feelings.

To make it more difficult, Evan Roberts, the famous evangelist—who always travelled with his three sisters—was at Tylorstown, attracting hundreds to his tents, weeping, wailing, frenzied with religious fanaticism; and if I had a semblance of a black eye people would go to the other side of the road to avoid me. Fighting was made a deadly sin by Evan Roberts!

It was a strike, when my first son was a few weeks old, that finally healed the breach which threatened to drag on for years. Not only was the money I had saved out of fighting supplying us with food where other families were lacking it, but I was able to earn more money when " off-work " than I had during full time at the pit. 'Lisbeth finally gave grudging approval of the booth fighting and for the first time I was able to devote myself to it without any outside worries.

I had two ambitions.

The boxing was the main one, of course. But the other was to leave the mines, and to get a house of my own. It was an almost impossible objective, but slowly I forged ahead with it, although the suggestion of buying our own house frightened 'Lisbeth. She was as well aware as anyone of the dangers of a strike, and if I sunk my savings into a house, where would the food come from? Despite my wins it was desperately hard to believe there was a regular way of earning money, other than the mines, and an engagement to box once a week for two pounds having lasted only one month made 'Lisbeth naturally sceptical !

But finally we made the plunge.

For the first time in my life I had a house of my own—a five-hundred-pound property, financed by the Club, or local Building Society, where I repaid two pounds ten shillings a month, some half of which was interest—with a *bathroom*. That was a triumph. I could see the past, the dirty, untidy hovel in which I had been born and bred, the dependence on the management and the landlord, quickly disappearing. A house of our own, a baby of our own, and general living conditions above the average. It was little short of a miracle.

Even 'Lisbeth began to admit freely that we had to thank boxing for it.

Not long after we bought the house, 'Lisbeth insisted on looking after my younger brothers and sisters. My home had broken up, and my mother also lived with us for a few months. Imagine a new wife, under twenty years old, looking after a family of eight !

Even that had its humours.

One of my sisters was being cared for by the Board of Guardians. 'Lisbeth wanted to get the family all together, and asked to be given care of the child. The Board met to consider the application : several oldish men and two women. Most of them were opposed to fighting (opposition was fiercer in those days) and 'Lisbeth was the wife of the notorious " Tylorstown Terror."

After a lot of questions and answers, aimed to discover whether we could afford to carry the extra expense, the Chairman eyed 'Lisbeth with some sympathy.

"But how can we be sure, Mrs. Wilde, that you and your husband are fit people to look after a child of this age?"

"And why shouldn't we be?"

"Well now," said the Chairman, "we've heard that your husband knocks you about, and if . . ."

"Knocks me about, does he?" flared 'Lisbeth. "I'd soon show him if he tried!"

And the board unbent enough to laugh at the fiery declaration, and raised no more objections. Soon we had the whole family under one roof.

. . . . .

Looking back over thirty years it is not easy to get facts in their right order, particularly of fights where there were no records, and no notices in the Press. Not that I ever collected press reports, to my grief now. My first big fight, with Sid Smith, came soon after my last fight for some years for Jack (John) Scarrott. Scarrott was a grand fellow, and for fifty years and more he carried his booth throughout the mountains and valleys of South Wales. Among boxing enthusiasts he was wholeheartedly popular, and he had some of the finest boxers in the world through his hands. A boxing booth is the finest training ground for a fighter. He's *got* to win to last.

Jim Driscoll and Johnny Basham—both afterwards good friends of mine—went through his booth, and it was at Porth Palace Cinema that I realised my first boxing ambition—to give an exhibition with

Freddie Welsh. I had idolised Freddie, and I did considerable damage in the three rounds with him. My reward was five shillings, and when I repeated the effort, soon afterwards, I had another five shillings, and some black looks. I was disappointed : I could hardly be expected to understand how damaging it was for a boxer with a reputation failing to show up a boy skeleton.

There were queer mixtures among the patrons of the booth, and I'm afraid I caused Jack quite a lot of embarrassment, once I had convinced him I could handle men twice my weight. My introduction to him seems funnier now than at the time.

Scarrott had a bluff way with him. I remember him glaring down on me when I asked for a job at the booth.

" All right, me boy, all right ! Go round the back of the tent, and stop the other lads getting in underneath, there's your job ! "

Obediently I trotted round the back. First one, then another youngster came up, looking on me as a kindred soul and expecting no opposition. I had to start a fight with one and before I knew where I was a dozen of them had started to mill towards the tent, and with my back towards it I was having the stiffest ten minutes of my life. Boys went down like ninepins, the crowd grew rapidly, youngsters joining in and older men roaring at the spectacle. But Jack Scarrott's roar terrified my opposing army at last and scattered them.

Jack was not a big talker, but he transferred me from a guard at the back to a boxer at the front. He made disparaging remarks about my skinny arms and

legs and it was true that the gloves looked like pil-
lows. But the trouble came from well-meaning
outsiders.

Protests were made against allowing a " fragile,
delicate " boy to enter the ring, and Jack had his work
cut out to prevent serious trouble once or twice.
A riot was almost started when I entered the ring
against a twelve stone man, an experienced mountain
fighter. Roars of " shame—stop it ! " replaced the
usual hum of expectancy.

I don't remember the other man's name, but he
had a big reputation in the Pentyrch and Taff's Well
neighbourhood. Finally Jack silenced the crowd, and
offered the other a pound if he could last three rounds.
There was not much in the first round ; in the second
he left himself wide open, and I floored him with
a swing that sent him unconscious for ten minutes.

Soon afterwards a man of similar reputation was
indignant at being asked to box a boy. I was giving
seven stone, and there was some justification for his
protest. Jack, beaming widely, told me that he had
just fifteen seconds in the ring to feel indignant.

Against these crude fighters, a knock-out was
coming as a matter of course, and represented so
many five shillings, not so many triumphs.

There were some good times with Scarrott's booth
and I was in real earnest all the time. The fight with
Dai Chips finally sealed my bargain with Scarrott,
who soon afterwards asked me to go with his string
to Caerphilly. I agreed cheerfully, and it was here
that my wife and I walked over the mountains,
carrying the seven months' old David, before
fighting.

At Caerphilly another seasoned mountain fighter, one of the toughest of the grand tradition, was " insulted " at being asked to box with a boy he could break in two with one hand. Scarrott offered him a pound for every minute he lasted. After some argument—the fighter and his supporters suspected a trick—the fight was fixed. Double entrance fee was charged, but the fight attracted a big crowd despite that.

It is a queer feeling to enter a ring against a man over twice your size, to hear well-dressed men and women at the ring-side, protesting against a " crime," and to *know* you can do what you like with your opponent. The fight in question lasted long enough for two left hooks—or just five seconds.

Caerphilly first made me feel that I was getting known. I remember the crowd which arrived when two big fellows, having announced their disbelief in my fighting ability, threatened trouble.

" I'll match both of you against him one after another, without stopping," Jack roared, " and you can hold the stake. If you last four rounds between you, a pound is your money."

The first man lasted two rounds, for the crowd had to have their fun : the other lasted five seconds. What they, and many others before and after could not realise, was that their weight and bulk *helped m* , and their confidence proved their undoing. At all events, with Jack Scarrott I earned regular money, and locally my reputation was soaring. It was on the strength of this I later took courage to approach Ted Lewis at Millfield, but I boxed for Scarrott for some time.

These booth days were full of incident, and there was one particular night when a man insisted that my knock-outs were fakes. Finally a spectator held the stakes, and the sceptic, a hefty twelve-stoner, started.

After seventy odd seconds there was twelve stone of flesh and bone lying on the floor, out to all the world.

Coming round, he said: " What have I been doing ? "

" You've been boxing Jimmy Wilde."

" I have been boxing, d'ye say ? "

" Yes."

" And who's won ? "

" You haven't."

" I haven't, but that little —— Wilde couldn't hurt me."

" Well, I don't know about that ; you are certainly not on your feet."

" Who isn't on his feet ? "

" You aren't."

" Then where am I ? "

" You've been knocked out."

" You're a —— I haven't started with him yet ! "

Jumping to his feet, the fellow made a dart at me, shouting : " Let me get at him ? " I side-stepped, and the enraged fellow dived right through the ropes and became unconscious for a second time.

A bucket of cold water, however, soon revived him, and with a disgusted look on his face he walked from the booth.

Yet another startling climax came after I had knocked another disbeliever out. Unfortunately the knock-out was not good enough, for the victim suddenly sprang to life and went berserk. Referee, spectators and doorkeeper all suffered, but the crazed man (as he seemed) returned to the ring apparently docile, and then lashed out at me : he could hit hard ! But immediately afterwards he collapsed, and I was getting worried lest he had been seriously injured when a bucket of cold water revived him.

He wanted to know when the fight was to start, and it took half an hour to convince him that he had rushed round the booth. Saddened and bewildered, he decided not to demand another chance to earn his money.

A few years afterwards, in 1916, I saw Scarrott again. By that time I was the English fly-weight champion, and holder of a Lonsdale belt. The dream of early youth had materialised. But it was grand to see Jack, although it was strange to accept an offer to fight for him. It was at the Tredegar fairground, Pontypridd, and Scarrott asked me to box four hours for him—*four hours !*—for a purse of forty pounds. I seemed to be back in the old five shilling days when I put on the gloves, but the welcome I had from the crowd warmed my heart.

In three-and-a-half hours, without taking the gloves off, I had nineteen knock-outs to my credit. Then half an hour's rest, and another four. The booth had been emptied for the interval, and another admission fee was charged, but I think it was more crowded than for the first show, and I have rarely known a crowd rise to me as that one did. There are more rewards in boxing than the big purses at stake.

Twenty-three knock-outs, all under sixty seconds, in four hours. It does seem absurd, doesn't it? But I proved during that hectic evening that booth-boxing had lost its old charm. The battle against a fully-trained man with a reputation as good as my own had far more interest, and that was the last time I worked for Jack Scarrott. But Scarrott, in the early days, had helped to make me, as he had helped to make many other champions. Little known, hard-working, certainly not wealthy, it is Jack and his fellow booth owners who prepare the champions of the boxing world. I have always believed the booths get too little attention, and that many world-beaters in the making never get more than a pound a fight.

★

THE BIGGER HORIZON

MEANWHILE I HAD MET TED LEWIS, LATER TO BE MY
manager and greatest friend, by forcing myself on him.

He was the manager of the Millfield Athletic Club,
run by two promoters named Williams and Gibbons.
It was a reasonably big concern and there was usually
a full crowd to watch. One went along and asked for
a fight, and for a licking you got no purse at all.
At the time I was six stone six pounds. Mining
life had not left a great deal of colour in my cheeks,
and I met with the usual scorn when I approached
the outside of the club. Two attendants first laughed,
and then threatened violence. I wished I could use
my fists on them, but I managed to keep my temper
and plead for an interview with the manager.

Ted Lewis came to the door at last. Ted was
also the official starter for track racing in Wales;
a genuine sportsman whose fairness has never been
challenged.

I shall never forget him as he looked that night.
Short, with grey hair which afterwards turned pure
white, a very fresh pink-and-white skin, and a pair
of pince-nez that made him look more like a school-
master than a boxing club manager. He was a little
deaf even at that time; later he grew stone deaf.

" I'm afraid you don't look the weight," he said, shaking his head. " No, put a little weight on, and grow a few inches, and come back again."

" I'll fight anyone at any weight," I replied promptly, " I've never been beaten yet, sir."

Lewis widened his eyes. I don't think he read bravado in the statement, although the attendants certainly did.

" You haven't, eh ? " Well, come in, and I'll see what I can do for you."

I missed the twist in the tail of that offer !

This was a bigger affair than Scarrott's booth. There were several hundred miners present, the air was filled with smoke, the lighting was only fair. But I was dressed and ready at last. Skin and bone slipped through the ropes, and a roar of good-humoured laughter went up. Well, I'd been used to that kind of ridicule, and I had also seen many men look as my opponent did, a middle-weight who obviously thought this was a joke in the worst of taste.

People have asked me what I *thought* before a fight. Well, I don't know. If I knew my opponent, and in those early days I rarely did, I had always sized him up beforehand. And I pondered always on the quickest way of finishing the bout. But in the ring there was just my opponent and myself, and the only thing I thought about was each punch, each side-step, each swing, each movement, and the reactions of the other fellow. Concentration was (and is) vital. All things outside the ring were forgotten, as though they did not exist. My man would start a move ; auto-matically I would go to counter it, without consciously thinking. Yet there was some activity in the little grey cells. In the twinkling of an eye the proper counter, and the best way to turn the other man's move to my own advantage, came into my mind. But directly the second was gone the thoughts had to move to the next emergency. It was more intuition than active thought, the intuition that will make a motorist perform a prodigious feat to avoid an accident. The main difference, of course, is that the motorist gets it once while the boxer is at it all the time.

There will be plenty of fights described later, and I need not dwell on that first bout under Ted Lewis's eyes. It lasted about four rounds, and I was vaguely aware of the thunderous applause when the miners had realised I was not only lasting a round, but going to win.

Looking back, it is amusing how many of my early opponents grew infuriated at finding me on my feet after the first round or two, and made up their minds to finish everything with a whirlwind attack, leaving face and body wide open. I was conscious then of the need for impressing Ted Lewis, and I went forward as fast as the other fellow. Right, to the heart; left, to the stomach; a chin jutting forward—out!

" So you still haven't lost a fight," said Lewis musingly, and I found his grey eyes strangely disconcerting behind those glasses. " Don't they call you the Tylorstown Terror, Wilde ? "

" Yes, but I've had nothing to fight yet," I said.

" You'll have plenty," promised Lewis. " How do you manage to punch like that ? "

I shrugged. I did not realise the scientific importance of timing the blows so that the other man, rushing in, added his weight to my own. None the less it is safe to say that half the strength of my knock-out punches have come from my opponent.

" I don't know. I just do it."

" Well, just keep on doing it," said Lewis.

Like all the men connected with boxing I had met, he was not overwhelmingly enthusiastic at first. He knew too many young prodigies who had faded out. But I think he was the first man, outside Dai Davies, to see my possibilities. At all events bouts at the Millfield Athletic Club, with a purse of five shillings a fight, became regular. I would often get three bouts on a Saturday afternoon, and I developed the habit of finishing them quickly. This was chiefly because I wanted to get home to my wife and the baby, always with a half-pound of chocolate almonds and without any trepidation in case I had been discovered in a deception. The other reason, and from a boxing point of view far more important, was because I realised the need for hitting my opponent before he hit me. That habit grew slowly until it became a regular practice.

Some fate watched over us in those days. Adding continually to our small savings, with the house feeling like our own, nothing came along to make us dip into our capital. My dream, of course, was to say good-bye to the mines. It seemed as though it was rapidly getting nearer, particularly when Lewis came up to me one day and said :

" Well, Jimmy, how would you like to travel a bit ? "

" If it's travelling to boxing, better than any-thing ! "

Ted's characteristic little smile came.

"Fine, Jimmy! I've arranged for you to go to Edinburgh for the Powderhall handicaps. Five pounds and your train fare, my boy!"

Five pounds and expenses, and applause while earning it! This seemed like a miracle, and I began to travel regularly to other towns.

Lewis fixed a fight for the seven stone championship of England on New Year's Eve, 1912. Purse—twenty-five pounds! The crowd at the Victoria Athletic Club, Glasgow, for this bout with Billy Padden was a large one, worked up because of the Scottish celebrations, and more than a little unruly: I could use a stronger word!

Ted Lewis was the butt of considerable "wit"—how he kept his temper under the rain of insults I don't know—and I dared not give a ghost of a smile in the ring. I had never fought before a hostile crowd (should I say partisan?) like that. It was positively dangerous, and I was almost afraid of winning.

Billy Padden and the promoter, Dingley, were disgusted by the display, but it was all in the day's work. Moreover, I was concerned because Padden was a fully trained fighter, and I had been working in the pits seventy-two hours before the fight. Billy gave me more than enough to think about, and there was considerable danger of losing until, gradually, he weakened. Young Snowball, his second, threw in the towel in Round 18.

The victory was certainly not popular!

But no serious trouble developed, and when one of my seconds asked me what I thought of it, I said:

" Never again, that's certain."

" It was a beggar of a crowd, Jimmy, but . . ."

" Fiddle on the crowd ! " said I. " I'm not fighting trained boxers again without training myself. Either championship fights go, or I've finished with the pits."

" I'm glad to hear you say it," said Ted, and I knew that was the truth.

So, early in 1913, the step was taken and I left the mines. But I was extremely self-conscious when I visited the homes of working miners; after all, I was something of a pariah, earning a living with my fists. Yet there was never a suggestion of reproach and it was easy to slip into an acceptance of the fact that I was a full time professional fighter.

Soon afterwards, just before a fight with Young Nipper, when my name was getting fairly well known, I remember being offered—and accepting— two fights. I told Lewis cheerfully :

" I've just fixed two more matches, Mr. Lewis ! "

" Two what ? "

" Two more fights ! "

" You don't worry about anything but beating Young Nipper ! " snapped my manager. " I'll fix your fights ! "

Yes, Ted was always cool, detached, methodical, and forced me to take one of his habits at least; always looking after the job in hand.

A little later in the same year I had a tough fight with Dai Chips, and incidentally made a firm friend. Dai was a local boy and there was always a lot of arguments between supporters and relatives on our respective merits. Hitherto his extra weight had stopped a contest, but it had to come.

Dai gave me plenty to think about, and it was the most strenuous of my early battles.

About this time I was matched against Harry Brooks, at Manchester. I reached the small hotel next to the hall and wanted to sleep. How tired I was! But the hotel was crowded, and I had to share a room with another man.

He was nearly asleep and we exchanged no more than a few grunts, although I had an idea that I had seen him before. In any case I saw him again soon afterwards : it was Harry Brooks, and for eight rounds we shared a ring instead of a bed, without the opportunity of feeling tired.

About this time, too, came one of those changes that make women so incomprehensible. I don't claim to know much about them, but I did know that 'Lisbeth's approval of boxing was qualified by the money it was earning. Dare I say again that this was not greed or avarice? It was simply the knowledge that a family caught up in a rail or colliery strike knew starvation, and that fear was born and bred in the South Wales coal and mining villages.

That aside, 'Lisbeth started coming to the fights.

She seemed to find an enthusiasm for the hot smell of the ringside, the excitement, and the actual battle. I could occasionally distinguish her voice among the shouts from the ringside. As often I heard my son, David, for to get 'Lisbeth to leave him at home in anyone's charge was impossible. During rail-strikes we would walk for miles over the mountains to Caerphilly—where Scarrott had a booth—carrying the youngster in turns, for, try as I might, I could never persuade 'Lisbeth to stay at home. I had the good sense not to taunt her with this change of front.

Here again, however, it threatened trouble.

But before it developed Lewis had fixed an exhibition with Young Dando, a well-known fighter whose exhibitions were usually pretty fierce. 'Lisbeth was worried for the first time.

" Do you have to fight a man with experience like that, Jimmy ? He's said to be extra good, and——"

" Have you ever seen me the worse for wear ? "

" No-o, but—all right, let's go ! "

The Merthyr man, with a reputation to keep up, went into the ring at Pontypridd with the firm determination to knock holes in me. It was obvious from his manner, and as obvious from the way he rushed at me after the gong went. I was giving away a lot of weight and Dando knew that his reputation would suffer badly if he made a poor showing, although it was officially an exhibition fight.

With my wife getting enthusiastic, Lewis beginning to hold out hopes of a real career, I saw in Young Dando an opportunity that might firmly establish me. No exhibition fight I have ever seen or fought in could approach it. We were out for blood and we both got it. I think the chief difference which characterised most of those early fights was that Dando grew hot-tempered, while I was gifted with a detachment that made a fight no different from a real exhibition. The detachment helped me to show up the better of the two : I think it was one of the bigger stepping-stones to the championship. It was after that exhibition that the crowd roared :

" No—more—fights. Give us EXHIBITIONS ! "

I fought Young Dando in serious bouts several times afterwards, and he always proved himself to be a fine sportsman. In the Cardiff fight, which went the whole twenty rounds, he did not know how nearly I had failed to appear.

I had gone along to the booth, as usual. Alf Harry, a booth owner of Sketty, Swansea, asked :

" Fighting Young Dando this week, Jimmy ? "

" Yes, that's so," said I, and started to strip. I was half ready when Ted Lewis rushed in.

" For heaven's sake, Jimmy, hurry ! "

" Hurry—for what ? "

" Great Scott, boy, you're fighting Dando at Cardiff, and you've three minutes for the train ! "

Overcoat over underclothes I rushed to the station, scraping into the train at the last minute. In that Cardiff fight with Dando, which was awarded to me after twenty rounds, he floored me in the seventeenth and nearly had my scalp.

I'm afraid I often gave Ted needless anxiety because of a faulty memory. After a long journey from home to Edinburgh, before a fight with Easton, I went to the hotel, lay down—and slept !

My first thoughts on waking were that burglars were about. That was corrected when the door crashed in, and Lewis and Hughes fell into the room.

" What on earth is it ? " I demanded.

" Is the man crazy ? " cried Ted. " You're due to fight *in twenty minutes !* "

At the same period I first met Alf Mansfield and there have surely been few fiercer contests. I am told that it is still spoken of thirty years afterwards by the Leeds sportsmen who saw the bout.

But to go back. I was not too cheerful when Lewis talked seriously to me soon after the first Dando fight.

" Jimmy, you've a champion's punch and a champion's ring-craft, and you've got nothing to back it up with. You've got to put on weight."

" But I'm fit ! " I protested.

" I can't match you with the bantam-weights," Lewis protested, and when others added their pleas I tried to obey. But meat three times a day, and sometimes a pound and a half of meat at a meal, eggs by the dozen, and every trick of diet I knew or 'Lisbeth learned, took me no way past the six stone ten pounds. Lewis almost despaired, but he matched me at last against Young Baker of Liverpool.

Baker had a reputation not dissimilar to my own. Countless minor victories, no defeats, and no fights out of the ordinary. The bout was a six rounds one, at the Pudsey Street Stadium, Liverpool ; in reality an old barn. 'Lisbeth badly wanted to come, and I cheerfully agreed to take her.

But Lewis had other ideas, and trouble threatened again.

" Jimmy, you can't take your wife to the ring-side with you—it's absurd. Wife and baby indeed ! She'll have to stay at home. Will you arrange it ? "

Ted didn't know 'Lisbeth, but I held him in some awe in those days, and I promised. By every trick I could think of I tried to get her to stay behind, without saying why. And then—shame on me to say thank heavens, but I did!—young David developed a cold, and 'Lisbeth elected to stay behind.

Mightily relieved I caught the train, met Baker successfully and returned home. David Hughes (who handled the legal end of most of my business) had been with me, but not Ted Lewis, and I had no idea of trouble until I saw Lewis standing outside the house, his pink-and-white face wreathed in smiles.

" Why are you here ? " I asked him. " Is 'Lisbeth out ? "

" No, I am," Lewis exclaimed. " Jimmy, I'm ashamed of you, your wife *threw me* out of the house. Your manager ! "

" She did, did she ! "

" Now listen, it's all right, I haven't laughed so much for years," said Ted. " But you'll have to make peace between us."

That was not so easy as it seemed. 'Lisbeth was in a flaming temper, and it came out gradually. Lewis knew nothing of the fortunate cold, and had greeted 'Lisbeth with congratulations at her good sense in staying behind. Thereupon 'Lisbeth promptly and effectively bustled him out of the house to cool his heels and wait for me.

Well, that died down, thanks at first to Hughes' disgust at Ted's mistake, which amused 'Lisbeth. But despite his repulse Ted Lewis still disapproved of 'Lisbeth and the youngster being near the fights. As the baby grew older and could be left the problem resolved itself round 'Lisbeth. Finally Lewis worked at the difficulty with a cunning I had not suspected in him. A remark of my own started it.

" They get fine crowds at Pudsey Street, Ted, and I think they're increasing."

"*You* draw them," said Ted, and for the first
time I realised that I was acting as a big draw, no
matter in what humble circumstances. Having
made his point, Lewis went on :

"But it's so difficult, Jimmy, the fans don't like
to think your wife's there all the time. Don't you
think . . . ? "

Finally I agreed to try again. But I found 'Lisbeth
more obstinate than I had expected, and I was filled
with fears of my boxing career being ruined. The
argument lasted all the morning of the fight, along
the street to the station, and in the carriage. I would
not buy her a ticket, so she bought her own. Finally
we both got a fit of the sulks. I took one corner,
'Lisbeth went at the far side of the carriage.

At a station an acquaintance of mine who was
going to the stadium climbed in. How I hoped
'Lisbeth would not introduce herself !

The friend caused the damage. He leaned over
and whispered :

"I think I've seen that woman before, but I'm
blessed if I know where. Do you know her ? "

I gulped. That unavoidable direct question again !

"Perhaps—at the ring," I said. "It's my wife."

"Your—*wife !* " The word came out so explo-
sively that 'Lisbeth heard it. And the friend, not
unnaturally, found it hard to understand why husband
and wife should sit at opposite ends of the carriage.
'Lisbeth of course came up and joined in the conversation and finally the other man discovered the
cause of the trouble.

"Who said the fans don't like it ? " he demanded.
"They like you for it, Jimmy, and they're learning

JIMMY WILDE
Wearing the Lonsdale Belt.

JIMMY WILDE'S LAST PAY SLIP FOR A
FORNIGHT'S WORK
Out of this a boy had to be paid 2s. 6d. a day.

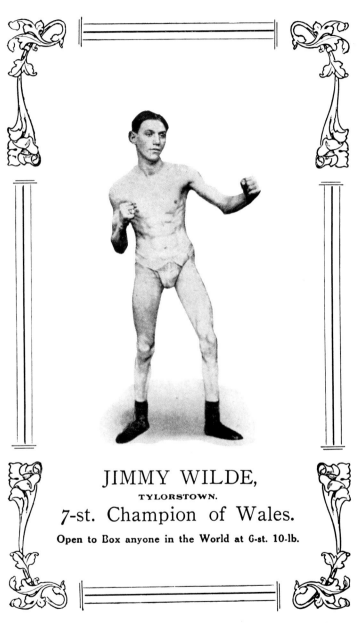

JIMMY WILDE,

TYLORSTOWN.

7-st. Champion of Wales.

Open to Box anyone in the World at 6-st. 10-lb.

JIMMY WILDE AT THE BEGINNING OF HIS
CHAMPIONSHIP CAREER

TED LEWIS
Jimmy Wilde's friend and trainer.

IN 1915. A SERIOUS CHALLENGER FOR THE
LONSDALE BELT

DURING TRAINING FOR THE
FIRST TANCY LEE FIGHT
Bob Downy, Jimmy Wilde, Bailleu (trainer)
and daughter Peggy.

ON BOARD THE *ADRIATIC*
AFTER THE TRIUMPHANT
TOUR OF THE STATES, 1921

(*Left to right*): Charles de Harrack,
famous pianist, Prince William of
Sweden and Jimmy Wilde.

BOMBARDIER BILLY WELLS TRIES SOME 'ROUGH STUFF' ON J. W. AT THE
ATHLETIC SPORTS, WEST BROMWICH, IN SEPTEMBER, 1916, IN AID OF THE
SPORTSMAN'S AMBULANCE FUND

Photo: Central News

AT SANDHURST, DURING THE WAR

to expect her. Tell Lewis he's talking out of the back of his neck."

I did, but not so effectively as 'Lisbeth. And Ted, who always retired gracefully when forced to it, threw up the sponge. 'Lisbeth was recognised as a regular fan, and I believe the chance-met friend on the train was right. I know 'Lisbeth's presence was always a thing of pride to me, but I wondered how many who saw her at the ringside would ever guess the trouble my boxing had threatened our domestic life in the early days.

I've been told that 'Lisbeth started the fashion of boxers' wives being at the ringside, and although I cannot vouch for the truth of that, I do know that she was one of the first to make regular appearances. Before the war women were not supposed to see anything but brutality in prize fights, and her persistence was in the face of general disapproval from the world at large. It is now difficult to show the revolutionary nature of wifely support at the ring in those days, but it should be remembered that there were nothing like so many women in the crowd as there are to-day. The large proportion of the fair sex at to-day's big fights is an innovation that would make the fans of pre-war days rub their eyes in amazement and probably open their lips in profane condemnation.

Just before this, Ted Lewis, David Hughes and myself were travelling to South Wales when three gentlemen of the card-sharping fraternity button-holed us. We suspected their game, but wanted a hand or two.

" Well—just for small stakes," said Ted.

" Fine, fine ! "   One of the trio, a large man with
a red-veined nose, started to deal.   " Going as far
as South Wales, gentlemen ? "

" Of course ! " said Ted.

Strictly to form, we were allowed to win, until
nearing Hereford they started recouping.   When
the train stopped, Ted jumped out ; I was the last
to remain in the carriage.

" What the devil's this ? " spluttered Veiny.   " You
said you were going to . . ."

" But not to-day," said I, " and we're choosey
about our company."

I was glad they kept their protests to somewhat
unorthodox verbiage, and did not try to show violence.

Later in the book there will be opportunities for
talking of the many famous sporting personalities
it has been my pleasure and privilege to meet.   I
did not, of course, find them gathered together in
a large hall waiting to meet me !   Ted would introduce me quite casually.   " Jimmy, this is Lord . . .
who's come to see you to-night.   This is . . ."

All this was at the Liverpool Stadium.   It was
dawning, somewhat slowly I'll admit, that I was
getting well in the public eye.   'Lisbeth would find
little paragraphs in the daily papers after unexpected
victories.   By now my great ambition had been
realised : I was free from the mines, and I had my
own house.   Then, prompted by Lewis, and inspired
by my own hopes, I started for the qualifying rounds
of the Lonsdale Belt, which had not then been won.
To get into the final bout would mean a London
trip, the National Sporting Club, all the crystallisation
of my hopes.

There is little need to recount the stepping stones to the first serious challenge for the title, but one night's work at the Oxford Music Hall does, I think, deserve mention. Harry Williams, the well-known promoter in those days, invited me to box two men in one evening. My opponents were to be Darkie Saunders and Bill Magnus, useful boys but not world-beaters by a long way. I forget whom I met first, but I know the two bouts lasted for five rounds, and gave impetus to the subject I am going to deal with in the next chapter.

CHAPTER V

★

OUTBURSTS IN THE PRESS[1]

IN 1913 THERE WAS SOME TALK OF A TOUR IN THE
States, and I was eager for the trip. Ted Lewis
was making arrangements with Charley Harvey,
who knew a great deal about American conditions.
Harvey had arranged many tours for English boxers
in the States, but he was pessimistic about my chances.

" There's nothing to fight," he told us one day.
" We couldn't get you a match, Jimmy."

" Well, I don't mind the weight," said I.

" You'd have more trouble than you do over
here," Harvey assured me. " If you had an extra
stone you'd be all right."

To go against the considered opinion of one of
the shrewdest men in Anglo-American boxing was
manifestly absurd, and so I resigned myself to con-
founding my weight, not for the first time. Just
a few pounds stood between me and a grand tour of a
new country ; it was difficult to be cheerful about it.

Les Williams of Tonypandy and Dai Bowen of
Treherbert were the " lucky " boys to go. They
would have had a successful time in America,
but they left for the States on the *Titanic*, and

[1] In many cases the press cuttings quoted are from papers of
which no record was kept, the bare cuttings only being available.
Mr. Wilde has, however, the originals of them all.

were among the hundreds lost in that dreadful
disaster on the high seas.   Had I been given those
few extra pounds I would have shared their fate;
so I blessed my size.   I sometimes shudder when I
realise how desperately hard I tried to make Harvey
change his mind.

Jim Driscoll, who lived at Cardiff, and whom I
knew well, was asked in that year by Ted Lewis
to second me in some of my fights.   That com-
menced a friendship which lasted until Jim's death
from consumption some seven or eight years ago:
there will never be a finer sportsman than handsome
Jim Driscoll, and there can be few finer boxers.

Driscoll seconded me when I fought Young
Jennings, at one time world fly-weight champion, and
won after eleven fierce rounds.   Few things have given
me greater pleasure than Jennings' generous remarks
after the fight, including:

" Very good, very good, Jimmy ! Keep it up.
You're a ha'porth of Sam Langford already ! "

Langford was perhaps the greatest " little man " I
knew about, and it was high praise from a boxer of
Jennings' reputation.

Meanwhile the days of big London fights were
drawing near.   I remember, by the way, that when I
first visited London I was aghast at the traffic, but
pestered Ted for a ride in a hansom cab.   Ted sub-
mitted at last.

" All right then, Jimmy, you'll have it ! "

So we climbed in and sat back : and I promptly
began to hate the traffic.   It seemed impossible that
our cab could get through the buses, heavy vans and
smaller vehicles without being crushed : every single

thing on the road seemed to make a bee-line for us :
I left the cab a chastened and wiser man.

Here is a " character sketch " that appeared about
that time—actually in April 1914 :

" We have been trying to understand the ' why
for ' and the ' which not ' of it all ever since Monday
last, when we discovered him at the National Sporting
Club, but Saturday finds us still wondering and our
brain (a particularly fine one) is beginning to soften.

" It was not until Billy Wells moved his right
leg that we became aware that the limb was
effectively screening so great a little man as the
Tylorstown pocket champion.

" At first we thought of asking Mr. Bettinson
whether the London County Council knew about
the little chap being out so late. A member of the
club, however, volunteered the information that
Jimmy had seen twenty-two summers.

" The point that has been exercising our mind is :
Why should ninety-four pounds of whipcord,
grafted on to a ' left kick ' and a ' right thunderbolt',
be allowed to masquerade under the disguise of an
innocent smile ? It ought to be seen to.

" We feel that many an aspirant to pugilistic
honours has been severely let in, or let down, by
this gay little deceiver.

" And what a nerve ! This tabloid world-beater
imagines he must be ill if he doesn't put his man down
inside three rounds, and his wife suggests a tonic.

" Our advice to any ambitious youth craving for
a joy-ride with Jimmy, inside a nine feet ring, is—
get fit and touch wood.

" This atom of Rhondda rampancy was not reared in the lap of luxury. He breaded his butter by delving for coal.

" It often happened that this wee miner was lost for a considerable time. His skill in wedging himself in cracks in the coal, or under a nugget of kitchen best, was truly marvellous.

" But Jimmy could not live on coal-dust alone. He dreamt dreams of larger worlds. In the wealth of his youthful fancy he saw himself standing over the prostrate form of Billy Wells, surrounded by bouquets, thrown by the cheering multitude.

" He took unto himself a wife, and the happy couple have presented the nation with a duplicate Jimmy who will one day, without doubt, provide excellent copy for the sporting Press.

" Jimmy is filled with radiant hope, realising the possibilities—and the great probabilities—of the near future. If he has any troubles, he tells them secretly to his homing pigeons, or to the friend of his bosom—one Percy Jones.

" If ever it were our fate to be recast, and given an option, we should unhesitatingly request to be started right away as a fly-weight champion— with Mr. Ted Lewis for our manager.

" Like ' Peter Pan ' Jimmy will never grow old, but we should imagine he will be ticklingly amusing when he takes to growing whiskers.

" Jimmy, boy, we take off our hats."

The reference to Peggy Bettinson and the L.C.C. has its own humour, for Peggy was the virtual dictator of the N.S.C. Yet a benevolent, if gruff, dictator, and one of the best promoters and match-makers of his time.

It was in May, 1914, that I met Georges Gloria, who at one time had beaten Carpentier. Again someone else's words will save my blushes :

" Poor Gloria. It was too cruel. The house laughed and kept on laughing, but it wasn't laughing at him. The amusement was all at Wilde. His amazing insouciance, the uncanny ease with which he did everything he felt inclined to do and the calm air of superiority with which he refrained from hurting Gloria overmuch at other times was one of those things which you had to laugh at.

" He is so small. He looks so fragile. He is such a child. With his pipe-stem arms and the weird twists and twirls of his legs, he might be taken for a wooden doll rather than a professional boxer. He will not even put up his hands save when he remembers that this is but an act of courtesy to which the other fellow is, after all, entitled."

A few weeks earlier I had been successful against another Frenchman, Bouzonni. Bouzonni was rugged and tough, and in the early rounds had gone all out. In fact many ringsiders (the fight was at the Liverpool Stadium) had been convinced that I had met my Waterloo. Actually Bouzonni had spent all his strength in the first three rounds, although had he managed to get home with some of his swings the pessimists would have been justified.

Bouzonni was groggy after a right to the chin in the sixth round, and when the fight finished (in that round) was helpless against the ropes. And how the crowd roared ! It was relief, I think, after the " scare " that Bouzonni had found too much for me.

It was shortly after the Gloria bout that a well-known boxing writer let himself go :

" But I have lived to see the greatest—absolutely the greatest—fistic marvel of this or any other generation. Little Jimmy Wilde is the man to whom I refer, and I can safely say that he has done more than any other man in the old or modern prize or boxing ring. I have carefully gone through the history of the prize ring from the earliest days— 1719 or thereabouts, but have failed to find any record or mention of a youngster giving away weight as Wilde has done, and coming off victorious. The nearest approach to him that I can find is Jack Broughton's favourite pupil, Ned Hunt.

" Wilde's wonderful work lies in the fact of his being but six stone ten pounds and giving weight away—a stone upwards to men of boxing repute. We know, of course, that a man of, say, eleven and a half stone can give away a stone or more to an opponent and not be heavily handicapped. Take, for instance, Sam Langford and Joe Jeanette, or Sam McVea or, to go further back, Tom Sayers and the Tipton Slasher, and Jem Mace and Sam Hurst. But we must remember that Sayers and Mace were in the neighbourhood of the middle-weight limit and were not men of six or seven stone. One great authority in the London prize ring said that a twelve stone seven man was big enough for any-thing on two legs—and so a man of six stone should

be big enough for anything on one leg ! But Jimmy
Wilde has proved himself big and clever enough
for anything on two legs within a stone of his
weight, and frequently more. The lighter a man is,
under twelve and a half stone, the less he can afford
to give away in weight, I mean to an opponent ;
and a bantam-weight ought not to give one fraction
more than a couple of pounds, whilst a fly-weight
must not concede more than a pound, and a seven
stone man cannot give anything. But the exception
proves the existence of the rule and here Jimmy
Wilde comes along with his six stone ten pounds of
avoirdupois and puts paid to the account of good
men and true who scale a full stone more than
the Welsh wizard. Never has such a thing been
done or heard of in the annals of the old prize ring,
or in those of the modern boxing ring, and so I
am fully justified in saying that Jimmy Wilde
is the greatest fistic marvel the world has ever
seen—and as such I raise my hat to him ! "

I think I had better get back to realities.
It was in July, 1914 (July the 23rd, I think) when I
was matched at the Liverpool Stadium against Art
Edwards. Edwards was popularly called an American,
although he was actually a local boy, who had lived
in the States for a long time. He had earned a justified
reputation, and what was more important, learned
many American fighting methods.
He was a whirlwind fighter, but he was comparatively easy to score against. Nevertheless he
floored me once, an unusual experience in those days.
He had, too, a tendency to hit low, but I often think

many of my opponents did so, simply because they were not used to judging distance against a midget. I was pleased with the comparatively easy points win that I scored and so was the crowd.

Liverpool had taken me properly to its bosom: I had fought there as much as anywhere, and the scenes before the fight were indescribable. Thousands were packed inside the hall while thousands clamoured for admission outside: all to see six-and-a-half stone in action! It was slowly percolating through my mind that I was becoming an "attraction" in the real meaning of the word, and it was a grand realisation.

Some indication of this growing prestige, and it would be absurd to pretend that I did not enjoy it to the full, was the activities of the sporting writers. Another is that I was being urged to turn sporting writer myself! I think it was in *Boxing* that I did actually break out, but before that—in August, 1914 —" Straight Left " sent me up wonderfully:

"A year or so ago I was at a boxing enter-tainment which for the first couple of hours fell very flat. It was one of those nights when the best-laid plans of promoters go wrong. So lacking in sparkle and life did the proceedings become that I prepared to go, thought better of it, and stayed. Afterwards I was very glad that I had acted on second thoughts.

"For I had seen one of the cleverest displays of real boxing that had come my way for many moons. A tiny, little fellow had been in the ring doing the most fascinating things in a supremely easy fashion; everything facile, nothing forced.

His name was Jimmy Wilde, from Tylorstown, South Wales.

" Since then Wilde has become one of the personalities of the English ring, and all the success that has come his way has been thoroughly deserved. For beyond a shadow of a doubt he has ability quite beyond the ordinary; there is a touch of genius in all he does, and genius is not so common a thing in boxing that we can afford to let it pass unheeded.

" Wilde rejoices in a multitude of aliases. He has been called the Welsh Wizard, the Mighty Atom, the Streak of Lightning, and so on and so forth. He has taken us all by storm. One has only to see him box to understand why. You see a thin wisp of a boy, with a waist of twelve inches and a bit, with arms like drumsticks, with a body of greyhound slimness. And you see him toying with men who by all the laws of physical strength should be able to put him in their pocket. And all the time he is boxing he carries an expression of infantile innocence, apparently convinced that he is doing the most ordinary thing in the world. I have seen him box several times during the past few months, and always I have received the same impression—that Wilde landed just how and when he liked.

" The secret lies in Wilde's wonderful judgment of distance and his almost uncannily clever foot-work. You have seen those boxers who dance all over the ring, and you have heard them described as artists in footwork; more often than not they are artists in merely their own opinion, and in the opinion of those who do not know. Wilde's footwork is of very different calibre. He never covers more ground than is necessary, and because of that he never tires himself. Always on top of his man, he shoots out that long left arm with exact precision, and whether he is boxing on the retreat or in attack he never wastes a punch.

" Watch him as his opponent comes in with the idea of mixing matters at close quarters. Wilde sidesteps, but he does not move more than a few inches. In a few seconds before his opponent can recover himself Wilde is busy again with his piston-rod left hand. His guard, without introducing the ugly ' smother,' is superb, thanks to his finesse and generalship.

" More than once I have been told that Wilde is not strong, but I think that it is a case of appearances being deceptive. When he boxes much bigger and heavier men he pushes them aside with a cool nonchalance that is almost laughably impudent. There is strength in those lathy arms, make no mistake about that. And when he hits he hurts. So does any man who judges distance so beautifully as Wilde does, for there is poise and balance behind the glove always—his punches are as clean and crisp as possible.

" As to his capacity for taking punishment I will not speak, for as a matter of fact I have never seen him take a hiding. But I have an idea that when that comes his way he will not be found wanting, for there is spirit and pluck written on his pale face. Wilde is a generous opponent, and one likes him for that : more than once I have seen him check himself when the man whom he was boxing was in distress. He would just as soon win on points as on a spectacular knock-out.

"Every day Wilde is getting better. In the Principality they think him a wonder and they know what boxing is in the Rhondda Valley. At Leicester, on Thursday last, he dazzled the locals, with his cleverness in his bout with Young Baker. So far his career has been in the nature of a triumphal progress. At the present time his services are greatly sought after. He is matched to meet Alf Mansfield at the West London Stadium upon the occasion of the opening night, September 20."

And perhaps it has a certain interest that I was persuaded to write, about the same time, in the course of a long article:

" KEEP COOL AND YOU WON'T MISS.

"Besides, so long as one keeps cool and collected, one is less liable to miss when one hits out. Of course, one misses at times, both when one intends to miss and when one has meant to get there. But as a rule one should be careful to miss as seldom as possible. Misses encourage one's opponents and disturb one's own chain of thought.

"Don't forget this, either way, because you can make the miss very useful at times. Say that you are up against a man who is boxing very cautiously, and who refuses to leave you any more openings than he can help. Well, then, don't be in any too great a hurry to take a too heavy advantage of such openings as may come along in the early stages.

" THE ADVANTAGES OF MISSING JUDICIOUSLY.

" Let fly a punch or so, of course, but be careful to miss. Make the punches look real not only to your opponent, but also to the spectators, because this will encourage him, and make him believe that you are not nearly so formidable as he has been led to imagine. He will then, in all probability, lash out at you with all his force, or at all events with a good deal of it, and every time he does that he is going to give you a chance to cross or to hook him.

" He may hit you, you say. Well, there is of course always that risk to take, but then if you are going to make up your mind that you are never going to run any risks, you may just as well decide that you are never going to make any great headway in the boxing game. For unless your opponent stands a fairly sound chance of winning, the match will be a very poor attraction from the gate-money point of view."

And to this I could add Jem Mace's dictum as a special emphasis : " Wear your man down with your left and then finish him with your right." Boxing has not advanced so much in technique after all.

In September, 1914, during the early days of the Great War, I fought my second fight with Alf Mansfield. Elsewhere I have given my sincere opinion of Alf, and in this bout he showed his inevitable

courage almost too well. Here again I can quote
a report of the fight that was published the next day :

"It looks as if there will never be a cessation
of the flood of praise that pours upon Jimmy
Wilde. You cannot have seen much in the north
of his latest victim, Alf Mansfield, and if that
is so do not put down this latest win as one in
which there was 'one more easy victim.' If
you knew Mansfield you would admire him as a
little fellow who is full of versatility and tricks.

"That is why he was rather easy game for
Wilde. The little wonder eschews tricks except
in exhibition bouts, and when a boxer is trying
some of those double-shuffle, triple-shift feints
that puzzle the man who is hot-headed to attack,
Wilde just steps back, waits until the spoof business
is over, and then settles himself down to a resump-
tion of the kind of boxing that makes him peerless.
Have you ever noticed what a simple boxer Wilde
is ? He does the obvious more frequently than
any man, with the exception of Jim Driscoll, I
have seen. There is a blow for a certain situation.
No boxer is so likely to try that blow as Wilde.
He just does what he should do, in a quick, plain
style that is only possible to the man who possesses
the coolest and quickest thinking of boxing minds.

"It was so in his contest with Mansfield, and
when the latter tried one of his more extravagant
attempts to draw Wilde into a false position, Wilde
would take one of those half-effortless steps back,
drop his hands, and look at his opponent as if
thinking, 'Why don't you stop that, and get

on with the boxing.' That kind of treatment made Mansfield understand that what had been his best tricks against ordinary boxers were useless in the case of Wilde; worse than useless really, for they meant waste of effort and no gaining of result except their effect upon the man who thought they would be of use.

" Mansfield was taught that he could not ' diddle ' Wilde, and even when he settled down to minimise the extent of his defeat he was still outclassed (an extreme word to use when referring to Mansfield) and he would only be left to wonder how much superior Wilde was."

The profits of this show, which was the opening of the new West London Stadium, were devoted to the Prince of Wales fund, and the winning gloves, as well as a dozen silk handkerchiefs which I had signed, fetched £18 5s.—no small sum. I remember Mr. Jimmy White bought one of these autographs, while that grand sportsman, Ernest Barry, followed suit and then resold it to the gallery boys—which brought the biggest cheer of the evening.

★

A NATIONAL SPORTING CLUB RECORD

SOON AFTER THE MANSFIELD FIGHT I GREW A LITTLE worried about my right hand.

The early days of booth fighting had demanded a lot of " punishment " for that right. It had been a case of stopping a knock-out blow with the fist or the chin, and I naturally preferred the fist. But some of the pounding it had suffered proved troublesome afterwards, and I had damaged it with Gloria. Now the right thumb was extremely tender, and it was discovered that the bone was slightly broken. This did not make it easier in the fight I had with Young Symonds, in an eliminating fight for the Lonsdale Belt, in November. But although the fight went the whole of the fifteen rounds, I was happy with the verdict. Driscoll's advice had proved invaluable.

" Straight rights to the stomach, Jimmy, and keep him away."

You can't damage a hand as much on the stomach as you can on the face, and the thumb showed no ill-effects. Young Symonds was really good, probably the hardest hitter at his weight that I had met, and one of the hardest ever.

And so the day of a serious challenge, against Sid

Smith of Bermondsey, grew nearer. The winner would be able to challenge the reigning holder of the fly-weight championship, and I was more than eager.

The first meeting with Smith at the Liverpool Stadium gave me the biggest crowd I had ever helped to entertain. We were both well known, with Smith having the more established reputation. Locally, of course, I was the favourite, but good judges fancied I had met my match—or I was soon going to. Here was the beginning of another vitally important scientific angle of my fighting.

By now, let me confess, I had both discovered and utilised the reason for the ease of some of my knock-outs—the strength of the other man meeting my blow, and, in the last few inches, putting in just enough extra power to do the damage. Before then, I had one aim: to get my man out as soon as possible; I had not realised that it was often wiser to let the fight last until a good chance came.

Knowing Smith's prowess, I decided it would be wiser to watch him in the ring. I had never seen him fight, but I heard that he adopted his own methods to counter those of his opponents. Well, two could play that game.

I think the early rounds were a disappointment to the four thousand spectators and I can hardly blame them. We feinted and sparred, but neither of us gave quite what was expected. Then in round five Smith came in and rapped me sharply on the jaw, enough to jolt me severely. Back I danced and Smith came in again, to follow up his advantage.

He hit me as hard as he could: something telegraphed that to my mind. *And he could not knock me out !*

With that conviction, I started to mix it. If the first rounds had been slow the later ones had the crowd on their feet. Smith was fighting coolly, scientifically, there was no hope of making him lose his temper and therefore his judgment. I put all I knew into the fight until the ninth round when I feinted for his ribs with my left. Smith dropped his guard to cover it, and I changed the punch to a right-hand for the jaw. I could see the surprise in Smith's eyes when it started, but he had no time to counter. He went down on one knee, and he was badly shaken. From then on it was easy, and after he had been down for nine three times, the referee stopped the fight.

That contest has an amusing sidelight.

My wife was at the ringside, as usual, and towards the end of the eighth round was surprised to see a man in grease-paint wearing absurdly long boots, take a prominent place. She discovered it was Harry Weldon, the music-hall comedian, who had come straight from the halls without changing, to see the bout. 'Lisbeth told me afterwards what happened.

" He came up to me after you'd won," she said. " He was introduced and then, before I could think of anything to say, asked : ' Who called your husband the " Tylorstown Terror," Mrs. Wilde ? '

" ' It would be Jack Scarrott,' I told him, ' and why ? '

" ' I'd like to meet Jack,' mused Harry Weldon. ' He must have a kinder heart than most.'

" ' A—a kinder heart, Mr. Weldon ? ' "

" ' I should say,' Harry said with his eyes twinkling,

'your husband's more of an executioner than a terror, by gum! Scarrott would probably call me only half daft!'"

Happily no one started calling me the King's Executioner.

George Graves, another comedian who has had his audiences in convulsions, came to watch me when I fought Sid Smith. Jim Driscoll chatted with him during the fight and had a conversation going something like this:

"They call him the 'Tylorstown Terror,' do they?"

"Yes," Jim was always suspicious of that kind of opening.

"Well, maybe," said Graves. "A flea in an empty house looks more like it to me."

Jim beamed; he could take a lot of that.

"Look at him!" exclaimed George Graves. "It's like a mother boxing ears, but a lot worse. He'd make a ringworm turn, would the 'Terror'!"

All of which Jim passed on later; but unhappily he could not quite imitate the comedian's droll way of uttering his jokes. Let those who imagine a comedian has a script hidden throughout his patter take heed of those impromptus.

But there is the unconscious humour, too, like the railway passenger (I have spent an unconscionable time in trains) who started talking about me, quite unknowingly, and finished:

"I'd like to see him box the Kaiser, that I would. That'd teach the . . .!"

And that after every conceivable means of punishing the Kaiser had been exploited, theoretically, in the carriage!

Soon after this Ted Lewis came to the Tylorstown house one afternoon, and after the preliminaries cocked his head on one side and smiled in a way that always suggested he had news.

" How would you like a sea trip, Jimmy ? "

" Well, a holiday would suit me well," I said hopefully.

" Holiday nothing ! There's a chance of a fight in Dublin, and I'd like to go over.   Will you risk it ? "

" Dublin for ever," I said without a proper appreciation of the dangers even during wartime in the Irish Sea ; and we arranged the contest with George Cullen immediately.   As a side-stake Ted and I had a wager of two new hats that the other would be sea-sick first, and the winning and losing threatened our composure after we left Holyhead : it was a draw, for we both lasted the crossing without giving in. Ted confessed afterwards he had been mighty close to failure.

" If you were as close as me," I laughed, " you felt a sick man.   The only way I saved myself was by looking hard at the horizon and imagining a submarine." Submarines and seasickness certainly did not go together.

The Irish were friendly, and there was no trace at all of enmity, although it was at a time when feeling was running high in what is now the Irish Free State. We did not have any cause to complain even of the traditional smell of the Liffey, and Dublin struck me as a graceful, pleasant, quiet city.   What a contrast with the truth !   The Civil War was fermenting then, of course, but to Ted and me, at least, there were no signs of it.   I remember that I had a terrific reception

—they can shout, the Irish !—both before and after beating Cullen in nine two-minute rounds.   And Cullen could not have taken defeat more graciously.

We arrived back safely in England, with neither submarine nor seasickness to boast, after a thoroughly enjoyable and trouble-free trip.   In Wales again we had our eyes on the distant horizon, too : the championship.   I think we lived for and dreamed about it.

All the time I was training at home, and Tylorstown was splendid in many ways.   The Workman's Institute allowed me to have a portable ring upstairs, while I spent considerable time at the billiard table below. But there were periods when I was away from the town indefinitely of course ; things happened as soon as I went to an hotel.

There was the case of the three boot-boys, for instance.

I was at a large hotel and the first interruption came in what seemed to be the middle of the night.   A piping voice calling :

" Your boots, sir ! "

" Leave them and go ! " I grumbled, and peace descended.   It lasted long enough at least for me to get to sleep, only to be awakened by a rumpus outside that must have roused the hotel.   I dragged myself from the bed and, prompted by I don't know what, peered through the keyhole.   Two boys were scrapping in earnest, but a harsh voice commanded silence and I did not need to interfere.

More sleep and then an insistent tapping.   Finally :

" Do—do you want some shaving water, sir ? "

" What time is it ? "

" Five—five fifteen, sir."

" Then get off with you and let me sleep ! "

Silence, but no audible retreat, and then :

" Your boots are ready, sir."

" Leave them, will you ! "

This time a slow dragging of footsteps, until I was drowsing again, only to hear another (clearly different) voice asking about shaving water.

That was too much. I hopped to the door and pulled it open, ready to let fly—with my tongue, of course. But there in a circle were three small, wide-eyed, nervous but adamant boot-boys, and after a moment's silence one said :

" There y'are ! I said we'd see 'im ! "

The price of fame on that occasion was a loss of two hours' sleep.

*   *   *   *

The record made at the National Sporting Club was not a boxing one, nor did I achieve it myself. My wife played a large part in it, and also in the preparations before the actual record-breaking.

I had not appeared much in London before, but I was matched with Tancy Lee for the fly-weight championship and the Lonsdale Belt, in January, 1915. By now I had it firmly fixed in my head that I could reach the top, but my confidence was like a shaky reed compared with my wife's !

It is difficult to give 'Lisbeth full justice without seeming fulsome. Perhaps if I just state the facts they will be good enough. Throughout the fifteen years of my fighting, she has cooked practically all my meals, helped me in all my training and had even—mostly in fun, let's admit !—sparred with me. We had a thin chain waistcoat made so that I could do her no damage, but if you could see 'Lisbeth's anger when I flicked the tip of her nose, you would be as amused as I was at the time.

Just as there had been trouble at first about her accompanying me to the fights, so, with my increasing reputation, did it grow difficult to fix training quarters with my wife in residence. It just was not done.

'Lisbeth knew the importance of this fight with Tancy Lee as well as anyone. And also she knew that if I thought she was unhappy I would worry more than about a hundred opponents. Consequently it was arranged that I should train with George Baillieu, at Porthcawl, and that 'Lisbeth should visit me once a week, with clean linen and everything that I would need.

'Lisbeth did not like Baillieu. He was a remarkably good-looking man, and I found him reasonably easy to get on with, although stricter on some points of training than I felt was necessary. I am sure that there was no " funny " work on foot ; it was just an unfortunate combination of circumstances.

I went into the training seriously for the fight, fixed for January 25th, 1915, for a £500 purse. With Dai Matthews, Len Rowlands and others as sparring partners, I did a lot of road work—always accompanied, by the way, by my dog. I had no worries. But on the Thursday before the fight I felt queer. My head was stuffy, my nose was running, I had the usual weaknesses of a severe influenza cold.

On the Friday when 'Lisbeth was due to arrive there was no news of her. Worried, feverish and with my feet in a mustard bath, I waited, sent urgent questions and messages, and finally threatened to go downstairs myself unless some news was obtained. I was sure 'Lisbeth was ill, or she would have been on time.

Then she came into the room, abruptly, flushed and angry.

She had been at the camp for hours, trying to get up to my room. Baillieu and his wife had told her I was out, for they knew what she would say if I was found as ill as I was, a few days before a fight. (It was Friday and the fight was on the following Monday.) It was one of the most miserable afternoons of my life. 'Lisbeth eventually left, after telling me, with tears in her eyes, that I would never be fit to box—and that was true enough—and vowing vengeance on Baillieu.

Everything possible was done to get me fit, but I was weak on my pins at the weigh-in, after I had travelled to London muffled up in thick scarf and overcoat, and afraid of catching another chill. I did not need to take my coat off for the weigh-in; Tancy Lee made the weight without trouble.

I knew that he was a fine fighter as well as a clever boxer, and for the first time I really approached a big fight with any kind of trepidation.

Not until afterwards did I learn that 'Lisbeth had told Ted Lewis and Hughes of the trouble, and had succeeded in persuading them to hedge some of their bets. They would otherwise have lost over £500. But what was more important was the pressure brought on me to call the fight off.

I had ample excuse, and any doctor would have

certified me unfit to fight. But at the threshold of
the really big career I thought it impossible to back
out. I had never missed a fight in my life.

"You haven't a chance!" Lewis said. "Not a
chance in a thousand, Jimmy. Be wise and call it
off."

"Sorry, Ted," I told him. "I'm fighting."

And that was about the limit of my conversation
that day. I must have said "I'm fighting" a thousand
times. Everyone in any way connected with me
and the fight tried to dissuade me, but I felt that I
would be doing myself far more harm by withdrawing
than by putting in an appearance. The fans would
be disappointed, the National Sporting Club would
feel that I had let them down, Lord Lonsdale and
Mr. Bettinson—of whom more later—would not
be able to trust me to keep my commitments.

Keeping my engagements was a fetish with me,
and it still is. Looking back, I am astonished at
the number of fights where no contract was signed,
by me at least. Ted Lewis, of course, had a reputation
second to none. If he said I would be ready at a
certain date, then it was as good as a written contract, and in some cases better. I had to keep faith
with Ted; on a mutual trust our association had
been founded, and it had to remain.

'Lisbeth tried bullying at last, threatening to give
the news out.

"Jimmy, I won't let you do it! It's crazy and
foolish, and you aren't giving your backers a chance.
Don't you see how it's impossible?"

"I'm—fighting," I said.

I think everyone gave it up after 'Lisbeth failed to

make me change my mind, but I was, if anything, in worse shape when I was finally getting ready for the ring than when I had weighed in. I could not stop shivering in the dressing-room, but with the tapes going on my fists, the familiar appearance of the seconds, the anxious Ted, I felt better. And outside 'Lisbeth was probably feeling better now the time had come.

The roar when I stepped into the ring helped me.

Tancy was already there, grim and daring to look at in his corner. He was as rugged as any man I have met, and could take any amount of punishment.

The formalities were quickly over, and I felt hot-eyed as I waited for the gong. Tancy Lee, one of the finest fighters to come out of Scotland, was looking fresh and fit; I wondered whether I could lift my hands to start a pretence of fighting.

I think sheer doggedness, the old habit that had always kept me on my feet, were my only advantages in that fight. I had not even the comfort of knowing 'Lisbeth was there, for Peggy Bettinson had been adamant against women being in the N.S.C.— then at Covent Garden—during a fight. Somehow I kept on my feet; they told me afterwards that there were moments when I fought back with something like fire, but they must have been few. Tancy Lee was fighting right at the top of his form, and he would have severely tested me had I been really fit.

I heard afterwards, of course, that I would have beaten him easily, and that I would never have stood a chance. The old contradictions went flying round, but the general verdict was that Lee had proved himself a better man, cold or no cold. For my own part, I wished the story of the illness had not got round, but I suppose it was best for my reputation. It was a palliative for my supporters.

I cannot tell you much about that first fight for the title. I know that after seventeen rounds I saw my seconds come through the ropes, for the referee had stopped the fight; and I was glad. I was not alert enough to be sorry I had lost. But of the battering I received, lacerating my lips badly, the right that Lee landed to my left ear caused the most damage.

It was as though a steam hammer had hit me. My head rang. I went on in a daze. And the ear started to swell.

During my earlier fights I had rarely been marked, but Lee had made up for it with a vengeance. The swelling continued and would not stop. Lewis and others got me to my room in the Club, pulled me round somehow and then tried first-aid to the ear.

It was then, and not in a delirium, that I started to shout for 'Lisbeth. I wanted her there, and I knew that she could perform the miracles that the others failed. I struggled to get off the bed, even threatened to throw myself out of the window. Of course, tradition was against me. A woman had never slept for a night at the National Sporting Club, and the request seemed outrageous. But I must have made them believe I was suicidally intended, for they went into action. Finally Mr. Ralph Lyle, the well-known Cardiff sportsman, agreed to go round for 'Lisbeth and the rules were relaxed. 'Lisbeth spent the night there.

What 'Lisbeth must have thought when she saw me, lips smashed and one ear hanging from my head like a toy balloon, I don't know. Lewis was trying to get it down by probing with a pen-knife ! I had not the strength to answer 'Lisbeth but I do know that I felt much easier shortly afterwards.

She told me that Lyle had been heard walking along the hotel corridor, whispering : " Which is No. 11, which is No. 11 " until 'Lisbeth heard him, and hurried out without dressing, except for a coat over her night-clothes.

Well, there it was.

Folk at Tylorstown were sympathetic, and my four sisters met me at the station ! But for the first time in several hundred fights I had a real taste of my own medicine, and although it was not palatable I knew, on the night, that Lee deserved the victory. My worry was the possibility that it would put an end to my career. Defeat was magnified out of all proportion ; it seemed synonymous with complete failure. But the ego in me refused to be quieted. I believed I could beat Lee, even on his form that night, and at least one thing had happened for which I was thankful.

I sometimes wonder whether it did not prove my real strength in later fights.

There was no more nonsense about training. I trained at home, or at least with 'Lisbeth to do the cooking—even in America, a few years later.

It was then, as a matter of fact, that I first took seriously to golf, and Bombadier Billy Wells was one who warmly recommended it. The doctors, too, suggested far more open-air work, and thus I started a hobby that has grown more and more important. Golf is first-class exercise and I had some glorious times on the Mid-Rhondda links, near my house, playing as many as three rounds a day.

There is something about the air up there that keeps one in the pink of condition. In fact I think the habit of living in the open helped to make me.

When 'Lisbeth had recovered from her anger she agreed there was something funny in the fact that she had been the only woman to sleep in the tradition-filled National Sporting Club. That was the record she shattered.

The old Club, hoary with tradition, has gone. There was something about the old Covent Garden building that seemed redolent of boxing, and I am one of thousands who have regretted the change, inevitable though it was. But the new premises at Earl's Court will slowly get the atmosphere, large though they are, for the Club patrons and officials are as keen as ever, the surest indication of the Club's future.

The more intimate shows are held in the Splendide Hotel, Piccadilly, where no recognised officials take part—as the hotel has no licence—and the fighters are tough youngsters who fight until the manager, on whom resolves all duties, decides they need a rest. Not so far removed, when one pauses to think, from the days of bare knuckles, and the mountain fighters of my own home country.

★

THAT CHAMPIONSHIP

NOW IT WAS A QUESTION OF A COME-BACK.

I did not realise how battered I had been, but I did discover that it was going to take months to get me really fit again. The ear was the trouble. I felt fit enough and I trained hard, but until the ear was fully mended, I dared not go into the ring.

Jim Driscoll, who had graduated through the " Scarrott University," came down to do some sparring with me. Jim was a friend with little to say, and a firm faith in " the Tetrarch "—for I was getting overloaded with nicknames now. About the same time, I met Benny Williams, who wanted to train me. 'Lisbeth liked Benny, who was a small downright man, well known in boxing circles, and very unlike Baillieu. Benny trained me for a long time, and I don't think either of us ever regretted linking-up. Benny led a man into training, Baillieu and a great many others were inclined to drive.

It would be about this time that 'Lisbeth and I grew friendly with Charlie Austin and his wife (Charlie, need I say, is the renowned comedian). He invited us to his house-boat, on the Thames near (I think) Maidenhead. It was a pleasant fortnight, although I could not join the others in swimming. Any work in the water slackens the muscles and swimming is a sport no boxer can afford to indulge in, whatever the weather.

While I had been "convalescing" Tancy Lee had come to grief against the Devon boxer, Joe Symonds. I had beaten hard-hitting Joe in November, 1914, when I had avoided his famous and deadly left hooks by contracting my stomach just enough to make him miss. Symonds made the most of that punch, and he was an aggressive fighter, but I had no reason to fear him. Nevertheless he defeated Tancy fairly easily, and it was rumoured that he had done as much damage to the Scotsman, if not more, than Tancy had done to me. I hungered after a fight with the new champion, and Ted Lewis was equally keen.

Ted had a way with him. That soft, easy smile, the quiet words, the little trick he had of turning his ear towards you when you spoke—caused by his deafness. His silvery hair was as famous in boxing circles as his reputation. That reputation was proved when, after long negotiations, we met gruff Peggy Bettinson and a bout was arranged.

The manager of the N.S.C. was never a man to talk or argue a great deal ; as likeable a sportsman as ever lived, but to keep an even balance at the Club he had to be firm. Obviously he bore no malice against 'Lisbeth for gate-crashing, and after referring humorously to that incident, he said casually :

" Are you ready to fight Symonds for the championship, Jimmy ? "

Was I !

" Whenever you like," I said promptly.

And, without an agreement, but on Lewis's simple undertaking to appear, coupled with my own, the fight was fixed for February 16th, 1916, with a five hundred pounds purse put up by the N.S.C. Committee.

'Lisbeth was in the kitchen when I got home, and she needed only to glance at me to know how things had gone.

" Now they'll see the real Jimmy Wilde, that they will ! " She was far more excited than I at the prospect, but inwardly I was on tenterhooks. I could not rid myself of the feeling that my prestige had suffered a severe blow at Tancy Lee's hands, although getting the new championship fight should have shown me that plenty of good judges had ample faith in me.

That faith was a big thing. I have not had many opportunities of saying so, but the belief that others had in me helped me to gain the confidence that proved so valuable. I have never been greatly perturbed by adverse, even hostile criticism—and in America as well as England I have met some— but I should probably have been much more worried without the solid backing that always came my way.

Living at home, training with Benny Williams, finding a bunch of sparring partners who came up smiling no matter how hard I went for them—and for that fight, especially, I put everything I knew into the sparring bouts—I approached the second bid for the championship in a very different frame of mind. That nightmare period at Porthcawl seemed far away. My ear was what an ear should be like—thanks to my wife's treatment as much as anything, including frequent bathing with hot milk, the finest cure for a swollen ear. This time I felt as confident as I had ever done.

The Rhondda Valley showed me the same faith as Ted Lewis, Hughes and the others. Hundreds travelled up for the fight, and it was like being at home. The weigh-in went off without trouble, and if I had a regret it was that 'Lisbeth could not be at the N.S.C. ringside. But the gods had relaxed once; to expect more was to call their anger. John Douglas was refereeing, Jim Driscoll was my chief second. Everything set fair for the night of February 14th, 1916.

Symonds, not unnaturally, tried to make use of his extra pounds in clinches, but Douglas vetoed it promptly, and Symonds proved his worth by keeping out of the hugs. But before getting to the " fight proper " let me try and tell you what I was thinking before I entered the ring.

This was the first championship fight that I had had, feeling at my best. I *knew* that I would never be fitter, and was unlikely to have such opportunities in training as I had with Driscoll. Mentally I, was contented; nothing had happened to irritate or anger me during training; as a matter of fact I could never understand why so many tempers were lost in the ring, and particularly in training camps. I think that was in a large measure due to the serenity of my closer friends, Ted Lewis and 'Lisbeth in particular.

In a few minutes I would be stepping through the ropes, into sight of one of the biggest and most critical crowds I had ever fought before : kings of the ring would be there, boxers of every age, weight and fame. Personalities such as Lord Lonsdale, C. B. Cochran, stage stars and social celebrities. Peggy Bettinson, of course, as gruff and direct as always. Yet if I had a thought about them, it was to hope they had a good show. The one man who really occupied my thoughts was Symonds.

Here was a tough, sturdily built fighter—I use that word deliberately, but with no disparagement to Joe's boxing ability—with a record better than my own, for he had fought in more big-money fights, and knew opposition that I had only heard of. During the interval I had fought and beaten Tommy Noble at New Cross, after a grand fight, but where, frankly, I thought I had kept something to spare all the time. Noble was just that shade slower that mattered. Joe Symonds had comfortably beaten Tancy Lee, who in turn had plastered me badly—they were facts, and side-reasons could not be considered too strongly. And, in addition, Joe turned the scales at about eight stone against my own six stone ten pounds, giving him over a stone advantage in weight, while he was called, with good reason, the " Devon Fighting Machine." He had never broken down.

As far as I could I had studied his methods, with a view to getting my own vital hits in by taking advantage of his likely attacks. I knew his power, and I knew my own. Frankly, it did not occur to me that I could lose : the only question that I asked myself was how long it would take to win. Again the confidence created by so many things helped me immeasurably. The betting odds of two-to-one on me helped, too.

In the first round, after a little clinching and John Douglas's warning, Symonds caught me with a right to the eye that practically closed it up. It gave him the little extra heart that he needed for full confidence, and he would not leave me alone. Light-weights (I mean the whole range under middles) do more hitting than the heavier classes, making a fight a better spectacle, and I put everything I knew into countering him, and taking the offensive. I did not think about anything beyond the fight, and towards the end of the eighth round I fancied he had worked himself out. When he left his middle open I crashed in a stomach right that brought his arms down, found his neck and then went in with two-handed hitting as hard as I knew how.

Joe went down on one knee, and then raised a hand in submission. He had taken tremendous punishment, and had not been knocked off his feet, but I was glad there was no need for more hitting.

And then I heard the roaring. . . .

I remember grinning round as John Douglas lifted my arm, Johnny Basham darting into the ring and kissing me, Ted Lewis looking as though he had broken the bank at Monte Carlo, and the glorious realisation that the English fly-weight championship and the Lonsdale Belt were mine.

And was 'Lisbeth pleased? I have never known her more excited; to tell the truth, I have never felt so gloriously happy myself. Many championship fights ended my way afterwards, but the savour of the first was incomparable. About that time my glass of champagne habit started, after each fight.

Next day, in the Stranger's Room at the N.S.C.,

Peggy Bettinson presented me with the belt, and, said quietly :

" I'd like to congratulate both the winner and the loser for putting up one of the finest contests ever seen at the Club—and I think ever seen in the world."

Coming from Peggy, that was nectar.

The critics, too, were more than enthusiastic. How I wish I had acted on 'Lisbeth's advice and kept my cuttings carefully ! However, one relic, without date or paper's name—I think it was in *Boxing*—awarded me nine rounds to Joe's three, and said :

> " Never in the history of the ring has any boxer fought against *good* men fully a stone heavier than himself, with success."

Superlatives do sound good, at times !

Yes, they were grand days after that contest, and the scene in the Club after the fight was one I shall never forget. Hosts of Welshmen on their feet and singing *Hen Wlad fy Nhadau* (Land of my Fathers). And here is what we—Symonds and I—were reported to have said when we were in the Strangers' Room the following day :

> " I have never had to fight so hard before." (My words.)   " And I have never met a fairer opponent. Look at me ! Black eye and all—that proves how hard he hit me."

While Joe Symonds put the finishing touch to my contentment by :

> " I don't think I could have done better. The better man won, and I am satisfied now there is no

one above him. He is a great little fighter, and although a stone lighter he got me down until he became stronger."

Thank you, Joe !

I was even grateful for the black eye, perhaps the blackest I have ever had, because of one of the queerest things I have known connected with boxing. You must blame 'Lisbeth again. On the morning after the fight I looked at her, and there she was decorated with an optic almost as black as my own !

" What on earth have you been doing, 'Lisbeth ? "

" Doing indeed, nothing, Jimmy ! " And when she looked at a mirror, she was as startled as I. So were the doctors who examined an eye blackened without any blow.

It stayed for just one day and was completely gone the next morning. I know it sounds fantastic, but it was as much a fact as the kiss Johnny Basham gave me !

Talking of medical examinations, there was a queer business when I was arraigned before a crowd of medical men at Liverpool, all trying to discover where I hid my strength. They pummelled and pinched me, stroked and massaged me and kept shaking their heads.

One even suggested that I should be examined before the fights, in case I kept iron in my gloves.

They gave it up as a mystery at last : but is it so freakish ? Not one man of average weight and size in ten thousand could hit as hard as a fairly good middle-weight boxer ; that seems to me to be on the same principle : there are exceptions to all weights, abnormal conditions everywhere.

So another ambition was attained, another landmark reached, and I was anxious for new fields to conquer. The Press was talking of me as a " wonder-fighter," queer stories circulated about the freak-boxer, but the truth is very different. I boxed because I loved it, I could hit because nature had given me strength, and the mines—tunnelling in those narrow places—had increased it. Although I had little enough technical training, few men could have taught me the essentials better than Dai Davies, who, I think, was prouder of me than any other man ; and he had cause to be for I owed him so much. As for fighting theories——

You know how I liked to use my opponents' weight. I also found a great advantage in an exceptionally long reach, for my general size, and I had learned very early that the closer I boxed, the less easy it was for the other man to get in a really telling blow. And, for what it is worth, I always looked my man in the eye. Sometimes I think a sixth sense warned me from his expression what he was likely to do next. That habit accounts for the " uncanny anticipation " that I, and other good boxers, have been credited with from time to time.

But other things were happening, apart from boxing.

The Symonds fight, early in 1916, saw the first eighteen months of the War past, and the hopes of an early finish fast dimming. I wanted to join the Forces, although offers of fights were coming along fast ; for the first time in my life I felt the real ease of money, the thing I had dreamed of in the past. Yet neither Lewis nor 'Lisbeth made any attempt to stop me from trying to join the colours. The desire had gradually grown into a longing, frustrated for a long time by what must have been one of the oddities of the Great War. For I could not persuade the authorities that I was physically capable of fighting with the ranks !

I tried several times, hung about in draughty doctors' waiting-rooms to take a physical examination, but all to no purpose. It is almost impossible for me to believe that it actually happened : even with the Lonsdale Belt my proud possession, I was not passed as fit for active service.

At one time I had fought in Birmingham, and stood by a recruiting-box ; as I went up the Sergeant waved me away, but a couple of young officers, obviously out for a spree, decided I should be taken before the medico.

They fondly imagined they were taking me there by force !

But they were a genial couple, and I could see the humour of the situation and went along quietly.

" What regiment are you entering ? " demanded one, and there was only one reply to this.

" The Life Guards," said I.

That rang the bell for laughter and I consequently aped seriousness.

" Laugh, that's right ! It's the Life Guards or nothing ! "

" Hopeful little man," said one. " We'll see what we can do for you. Life Guards or nothing," he added with a grin.

However, the doctors threw me out (figuratively speaking, of course), and there was also another disappointment. It was not until a year later that I was " taken," and then for garrison service. In between whiles there were the unpleasant attacks from certain people and papers : there was even a story in circulation that I had been specially asked to join the Tank Corps, and refused. I wonder how many others, held up as bad examples to the public and advanced as proof of the need for conscription, had tried to join up and failed ?

I was able to help towards the various funds by boxing, attending different shows and auctioning gloves and other things after the fights. Nothing was too much trouble, enthusiasm everywhere was at fever pitch.

Yet reports kept coming through, of this man's death, or that one's serious injuries, fine boxers never to appear in the ring again. It was heartrending, and worse because of the knowledge that others took the brunt of the fighting.

But we just went on.

.   .   .   .   .

My house, on a hill near Tylorstown, was now something to be proud of, and it was more like a young farm. We had over a hundred pigeons, two or three hundred fowls, ducks and geese. Placed as we were, there were times when the weather made it difficult to get to and fro. It was during a fight that I suffered one of the severest blows I have had, although it happened two hundred miles away from me.

I won't pretend that I knew every bird on the farm, but I knew most of the pigeons, and I had two fine dogs, grand friends, who were always near at hand for training. Bess was a labrador-retriever, Jim a devoted Airedale.

My second boy was born during the great battle of Verdun, after which he was named. During the preceding months I had been matched with Tancy Lee again (more of that bout later), George Clark, Sid Smith again, Johnny Best and Johnny Rosner, the American bantam-weight. The four-round fight with Clark in March, 1917, was chiefly remarkable (and to me important) because it enabled me to win the Lonsdale Belt outright. There was also an amusing sidelight on the effect of Army discipline. I heard officers talking among themselves of backing Clarke, who had been winning everywhere. But it was more than I dare do to interrupt them and advise saving their money. Quite a lot was lost in the mess over that bout.

(Johnny Best is now a great promoter and matchmaker, particularly in the North. Another claim he has to distinction is that he made the first match at the Earl's Court N.S.C.)

All my opponents had pulled out their best: a boxer with a practically unbeaten record *always* finds his opponent at the top of his form, for the other man has everything to gain and little to lose; he can still claim to be the next best.

During a fight in London, however, I was, for once, thinking of something other than the job while in the ring. It was blowing hard and there were reports of heavy snow in South Wales. My house was in a bleak position, and likely to suffer severely during the storm: it was even possible that it would be cut off.

The journey back home next day was a nightmare, but nothing like so bad as things had been.

'Lisbeth's mother and sister had called the previous

afternoon but, on trying to get home, had found the going impossible and turned back. Dai Davies, alarmed by their non-appearance, had started from the village to find them, was himself overcome by the cold and lay unconscious in the snow for hours, until found by accident next morning, perilously close to death. And of the livestock at the farm—I called it a farm—only one dog, Bess, was left.

One dog, out of over four hundred living things! I was the most miserable man in Wales.

It was one of the worst storms that ever raged over the Rhondda Valley, and I suppose there was little use reproaching myself for being away, but had I had a presentiment of what was going to happen, I think I should have called the fight off. I wonder? Ted Lewis and I had never failed to appear, and it would have been a terrific decision to make.

Perhaps it was as well it was not put to the test.

Going ahead a little, there was another time when I might have been justified in refusing to fight—I'm glad I did not, for the fight did not materialise. Bettinson had arranged an open-air bout with Johnny Hughes, at the Kensal Rise athletic ground. I left Cardiff with 'Lisbeth in bright sunshine, wearing a straw hat—I have always liked straw hats, and I wish they had not gone out of fashion! But when we reached London it was raining hard. At the ringside Bettinson, Hughes and others were waiting, out in the open and making use of inefficient umbrellas, for the rain to cease. Everything and everyone was soaked to the skin, including my straw hat, and, incidentally, a new suit.

Finally Peggy gave it up in disgust and went back

to the station. It was a big disappointment to him, for out-door glove-fights were an innovation in those days. I was too disgusted to take 'Lisbeth's advice to get to an hotel and have a hot bath, but I escaped without a cold, perhaps more luckily than I deserved. The postponed fight, on which the N.S.C. lost money, I'm afraid, took place at the Club a week later, where Hughes, often called the " pocket Hercules," took a knock-out in the tenth round.

All this time I had my eyes on the world title.

But after the snowstorm episode and before the Kensal Rise wash-out, I had two important fights against challengers, and two train incidents worth relating. The first fight was at the Oxford Music Hall, then at the corner of Tottenham Court Road, against the renowned Tommy Harrison, of Hanley. Tommy was considered one of the best boys of his weight. Jack Callaghan promoted the contest and Eugene Corri refereed.

Corri was one of the most charming personalities in the ring, and one of the fairest. I remember when Pal Moore flapped at me in our big fight, Corri whispered :

" I can't caution him, Jimmy."

" Why ? "

" General Pershing is here ; it would look so bad ! "

The famous referee was very nearly perfect, yet he once made a mistake that seems incredible. In the nineteenth round of a twenty round contest he lifted my hand :

" Wilde is the winner ! "

" But there's a round to go ! " I whispered nervously, and Corri recovered as well as he could. I remember putting everything I knew into that last round, to make sure that the decision was not reversed.

Corri was extremely popular with all boxers, partly because of his scrupulous fairness, partly because of his whimsical, generous personality. He would approach us, sometimes, and borrow a pound or so.

" Now come and have a drink, boys."

I was often with the boys although my only alcohol was that champagne after a fight, and Corri's borrowed money would soon go. I had never before heard anyone say, as he lifted his glass :

" All the best—all the very best ! "

And I have heard it claimed that he was the originator of the phrase. Few people can have uttered it with the same spontaneity—he really meant it.

Poor Eugene Corri !

He died a few years ago, and many boxers— Bombardier Billy, Jack Bloomfield and myself among others—did not know he was dead until we learned of his funeral. If ever a man deserved a tribute from the boxing men, it was Gene.

Well, Harrison and I entered the ring at the same time, and were greeted by the band playing " Men of Harlech ! " It was bad luck on Tommy, but he grinned cheerfully. I can see him now, bull-dog all over, ready to fight every inch of the way.

That fight brings me to a point that non-fighters, especially those who claim to see something brutal in the ring, have raised often enough. How can one man batter another until his face is literally a bloody mess ?

Harrison was as game as they make them, but he had an unfortunate start. His nose was bleeding badly

after a couple of rights to the face in the first round.
Then I took his ear, and his lips. They were splitting
badly, and he lost several teeth before giving up in
the eighth round. People will ask, and did after
that : " How can you keep hitting at a man's face
when it is cut and bleeding badly ? "

Well, I don't know.

There is never any desire to see a man badly marked
—I have always hated being marked myself—but
there is a fixed desire to beat him, and the best and
quickest way to beat a man is to hit him hard on the
face. Harrison, in this particular bout, seemed to
lose most ideas about defence, and left himself wide
open. There was no enjoyment, let me repeat, in
knocking him or anyone else about the ring but the
job has to be done. I did not see blood so much as a
way of beating my man. The mind, when in the ring,
has to be completely detached from everything but
the knock-out, and the garnering of points. After
that particular fight the adjective " merciless " was
tacked on to me—in common with a hundred others
by now—and I suppose up to a point it was justified.
But if I saw a man being badly battered outside the
ring, I don't think I could stand it. Any accusation
of brutality, levelled against all boxers as a class
and not simply against any one, must be withdrawn
because of that fact. Only in the ring, when we are
thinking coolly and scientifically, does that merciless
" brutality " reveal itself. I do not think any boxer of
repute could ever be called a sadist ; surely no one
but a sadist could be at once cool and brutal.

But enough of the moralizing.

★

TRAIN TROUBLES

IF THERE WAS A FIGHT I HAD HANKERED AFTER, outside the apparently impossible world fly-weight bout, it was with Tancy Lee. I wanted to prove beyond all doubt that the previous result had been wrong. The weather was warm, for it was June, 1916, and the N.S.C. had put up a stake of £500 with side-stakes of £250. There was not much more money in a single bout in those days.

Shades of the five shilling fights !

Lord Lonsdale took the chair that night, for the first time since the beginning of the War ; another reason why it will always be memorable.

I have never felt more confident of victory, perhaps because I had, for me, a unique inspiration to win outside the prize-money. Tancy came at me hard and fast, but he found my lefts stronger than he had expected—a lot stronger than in the previous fight. He actually tottered once or twice when I raked him with my right. Then—a silly thing to do— I let him hit me once or twice, to test the weight of his punches. I was lucky, for they were not as strong as they might have been.

From then onwards I kept out of reach for a bit. Tancy must have been worn out, but he kept at me like a terrier, until I suddenly went in with everything I knew.

I did not think he could stand it, but he had a remarkable reserve of strength in that dour Scottish blood of his, and he even came back once or twice. The tenth round practically finished him, and he was weak at the knees when the gong went. In many ways this contest was a reversal of our first meeting : then I had been as groggy as he was now, and I wonder whether his thoughts in the first bout were akin to mine in the second. I had a keen admiration for the man's gameness, and surprised that flesh and blood could stand it.

His seconds threw in the towel after he had gone down from a right to the chin early in the eleventh round. It was over, and I had beaten Tancy Lee. 'Lisbeth pointed out, after I told her of the fight, that there was not a man who had boxed with me who had not lost at least once. It is queer how those little asides often mean so much more than the plaudits of the ringside and the Press.

Some idea of the difficulties that followed can be gathered by the quotation from a daily paper in February, 1916. The last paragraph serves simply to emphasise the amazing steps motion-pictures have made in the last decade.

"One of the Welsh visitors appealed to Mr. Bettinson to give Wilde early opportunities of other belt contests, as they were anxious in South Wales, he said, to have another belt ' for keeps ' to keep company with that which Jim Driscoll secured ; but the Club manager pointed out that the matter

was not in his hands or those of the committee.   It
remained for challengers to come forward with the
necessary backing and give Wilde the chances that
were so desired for him.

" That will be the new belt-holder's trouble—
to find customers.   There is no likelihood of
Symonds trying again, because it has been revealed
to him and his supporters while training for
Monday's contest that it hurts him to do eight
stone ; that, in fact, he cannot do the fly-weight
limit and be strong.   He was considerably worried
on Monday at the scaling ordeal and the incidents
connected with it, and his face and eyes indicated
the state of his mind for some time afterwards.
Some promising young boxers have emerged in
London from the eight stone division within the
past twelve months, but although they may look
champions in the ordinary way, they would be
of no use to Jimmy Wilde ; nor can Wales, prolific
as it has been in good little 'uns, produce a serious
rival to the ' Terror.'

" It is probable therefore that the champion
may have a long and undisputed tenure of his
championship—unless Tancy Lee once again
throws down the gage of battle.   There is the
possibility of such an event, it is said.   The Scottish
ex-holder had had all sorts of trouble in getting
down to weight for Young Symonds—trouble
vastly greater than that the Devonian experienced
on this more recent occasion—but he is going to
begin a gradual process of weight reduction varied
by actual contests, and if his supporters are convinced that he can be brought to the fly-weight

limit again in full possession of his strength and vitality, they will be prepared to back him, I am told, in another match with Wilde for a side stake up to £500.

" As was stated in these columns yesterday, Wilde's next contest is fixed for March 9, when he is to box fifteen three-minute rounds at the West London Stadium with Sam Keller, who will be allowed to scale eight stone three pounds at two p.m. on the day of boxing. It was hoped to get Wilde in the ring at Hoxton Baths before then, but owing to an expected little domestic event Jimmy will not be away from home until the March date. Mr. Jack Callaghan, however, yesterday secured from Mr. Ted Lewis the first call on Wilde's services subsequent to the match with Keller.

" Moving pictures of the weighing-in of Wilde and Symonds and of the contest later were taken by the Barker Photo Company, and an interesting sequel to yesterday's function at the Club was a visit to the Barker Studio in Soho Square where the films were run off, among those present being the two boxers and their supporters, Mr. A. F. Bettinson and the representative of the *Sporting Life*. The pictures, it may be said at once, are excellent, and were watched with great absorption as the story of the contest was unfolded round by round. The two little men whose doings were being portrayed sat side by side on a settee, and, craning forward, noted with rapt attention every incident of the struggle, now and again nudging each other as something of particular moment attracted their attention."

I stayed in London for a short while, after the Lee fight, to take part in the revue, *Half-Past Eight*, at the Comedy Theatre, but far more important to my mind was a visit arranged to the Houses of Parliament, on June 29th. Ted Lewis went with me, and we were greeted by a speech from the Duke of Buccleuch, in the Gilded Chamber.

Comparatively fresh from Tylorstown, can it be wondered at that I marvelled at the place ? It looked like a mass of gold, a positive dream of luxury and riches. I doubt whether I paid as much attention to the speech by the Duke as I should have done, and I left the Upper House in something like a dream, for the House of Commons.

Things in the Lower House were dull that afternoon, and there seemed to be some relief at an opportunity to pay attention to a somewhat bewildered boxer, for the political situation was extremely delicate. There was a big crowd, of all parties, and from both Houses, and my hand grew tired with shaking. (By the way, if you're going to fight in the evening, don't spend the day shaking hands too much : particularly if you have small hands).

It was strange that about the first man I met in the House of Commons was Mr. O. W. Owen, secretary of the Welsh Army Corps, with a little party of Welsh M.P.s. There was something like an argument as to my escort.

" I'll show you round, Jimmy," said Mr. John Hinds.

" Not you," called someone else. " Come with me, Jimmy."

" He'll go with me," said a third, and then someone

settled it by saying they would go together. I could agree with that safely and without being accused of favouritism.

Dr. Lynch, who knew as much if not more about the technique and theory of boxing as any man in the House at that time, had made arrangements for the visit, and it went off splendidly. I remember, near the main entrance, we met a crowd of wounded Tommies, in charge of a Mr. Wason. It was good to see their eyes light up, and I felt that boxing at home had something to be said for it despite my longing for Army service.

One man, walking with a pronounced limp, nearly fell over as he shook hands.

" Is it really Jimmy Wilde ? "

" Yes, I'm Jimmy," I smiled.

" It's grand to meet you. You wouldn't believe what a kick we get out of reading about your fights, Jimmy."

" Go on with you ! "

" But it's true ! " he assured me, and the others echoed his words. That was a grand moment.

However, we were nearly summoned for obstruction, so I was taken into the inner lobby and presented to a positive mass of M.P.s, including the then Labour Privy Councillor, Mr. Will Crooks. He had something of a boxing career, and we exchanged notes warmly, until someone chimed in :

" But a man as small as that *can't* be a first-class boxer, surely."

" Nonsense," said Mr. Crooks quickly. " I was taught boxing by a man just as small as Jimmy Wilde."

" There aren't any men as small as he," someone laughed, and the argument (with me standing hopefully by) almost grew heated, in a friendly way.

Among another group we met, soon afterwards, was a biggish man whom I seemed to know. He was introduced as Mr. Edgar Jones, the member for Merthyr.

" Edgar Jones ! " I lost myself for that moment. " Why, that's who it is—and you've often groused and grumbled about my fighting ! "

" Eh ? " Mr. Jones looked puzzled, and someone started talking about his secret past. " Where, Jimmy ? "

" At school, surely."

" School ? "

" Didn't you teach me, at Tylorstown ? "

It took some doing to persuade him that I was the diminutive and cheeky Jimmy Wilde of Tylorstown days.

" You didn't teach him his boxing," said Mr. Geoffrey Howard, but my old teacher had decided to take what credit was going then, and cheerfully said that he had taught me how to take a lot of punishment. He was probably right.

I remember being jollied by the Recorder of Cardiff, Mr. Llewellyn Williams, and playfully giving him a little demonstration while he called frantically for the more experienced Dr. Lynch to take his place.

It was a grand day, and I felt as much at home, after the first half-hour, as I should have done at Tylorstown. A host of policemen and minor officials helped to make my hand ache a little more. It was good to feel that the leaders of the country took an interest in sport, although I asked in vain for some tips to help me in the coming fight with Johnny Hughes.

Soon after that came some light relief.

We started back from Paddington for Cardiff, a little late for the train for comfort, and had some difficulty in getting a seat. There was one left, 'Lisbeth insisted on my sitting down, and I insisted on her sitting on my knee. But at the last minute a sailor, considerably overweight, arrived with his wife, glared round, obviously picked on me as the smallest possessor of a seat, and demanded it for his companion.

Here, incidentally, is something reflecting on the " brutality " of boxers. I know of only one or two who were ever willing to show their paces outside the ring and the training camp, and many of us will suffer any amount of insult and indignity rather than let ourselves go. After a protest or two, mostly from 'Lisbeth, the overweight sailor actually lugged me bodily out of the seat.

'Lisbeth's temper flashed.

" Hit him, Jimmy, hit him ! "

Seeing that there were many Welshmen in the carriage it is hard to understand how they failed to see the significance of that " Jimmy," but they did. I stuck my hands in my pocket ; what was the use of making a row ?

" All right," said 'Lisbeth, " if you won't, I will." And she brought her umbrella down with a thwack on the shoulders !

That, in the vernacular, caused it. In the general commotion, Ted Lewis and some other friends who had been in the next carriage, came rushing in. Ted grabbed the sailor's arm, and whispered frantically : it is not hard to guess what he said. The upshot was that, after the sailor had urged us back to the seat, he slipped out of the carriage at Newport and came back with a box of chocolates for 'Lisbeth. They were not chocolate almonds, but she enjoyed them, and the sailor proved himself a good loser.

On another occasion a drunken man entered our compartment, with a clergyman as the other passenger. The man's language was pretty dreadful, but I satisfied myself with asking him to be quiet, and kept the peace until he climbed out. Quite unthinking, I went to the window to close it.

And for my pains received a pile-driver on the nose !

The train had started off, but there were limits to what I could take, and that finished the drunk. With 'Lisbeth holding the door open, I hopped out on to the platform, presented the quarrelsome passenger with a single crack on the jaw and, after swinging back into the moving carriage, saw him stretched out and quite unconscious. I hope he was sober when he came to !

Later, we had a delightful letter from the clergyman, who had discovered our identity and had pleasant things to say about keeping an even temper, and teaching more volatile gentlemen their manners. Once again the little things gave a greater pleasure than many of the bigger triumphs.

Another train incident can be mentioned here. Jim Driscoll, Ted Lewis and Dai Evans, of Mountain Ash, were travelling with me to the second Tancy Lee fight. Two strangers were in the compartment, and professed their pleasure at meeting boxers of fame. We played cards and the strangers lost with grace, but annoyed Ted and Driscoll by saying :

" One thing's certain, gentlemen, we can put our men out quicker than the great Jimmy Wilde."

" That's so ? " demanded Jim Driscoll. " Then who are you ? "

" Strictly incognito," said one of them.

" Incognito or not," snapped Jim, " we'll match you any time you like with Wilde.

Broad grins on two faces, and the spokesman said :

" All right, but we'll have to arrange it with the Government first." And they said no more.

Ted and Jim cooled down. We were friendly enough when they left the carriage, but startled when one said cheerfully :

" Now I'll give you our names, gentlemen. This is Pierpont and I'm Ellis, with appointments to-morrow at Strangeways Jail."

Pierpont and Ellis, the Public Hangmen—the match Driscoll offered was one I was glad enough to miss !

I remember the others talking about it for the rest of the journey, but I had Lee to think about. Wilkie Bard was at the ringside, shouting the first bet that night.

" Three hundred to one hundred on Wilde, and easy money."

But I thought at times of Strangeways Jail.

Fights came and went. Tommy Noble knocked me off my feet at Liverpool, in the November, and lasted for eleven rounds that might have been fiercer, and of course the fact was emphasised in the Press. Only Tommy and I know what happened to send me down!

We had one diversion that might have been very serious. 'Lisbeth was zealous in looking after my food, but one evening before a fight took a chance with some prepared brawn. Now I have always been suspicious of anything not cooked at home, and I'm told that I lost my temper in demanding something different : luckily temper was restored when some fresh salmon was available.

A few hours afterwards 'Lisbeth and her mother, who was with us, started complaining about stomach pains. Our six-year-old David collapsed, and so did the maid. The illness—ptomaine poisoning from the brawn—lasted only a couple of days and had no serious consequences, but if I'd taken the chance with the meat, my fight the following evening would have been " off." Perhaps that was a rare example of an occasion when a lost temper really did some good.

Soon after this an undreamed of chance came. Zulu Kid, the American fly-weight champion, was coming to England. Jack Callaghan, a good-humoured sportsman and one of the finest promoters in the game, promoted a fight for the world championship, and the contest was fixed at the Holborn Stadium. What dreams I had during training are hard to remember, but those of victory loomed largest. The world championship——

Would it be more than a dream ?

.   .   .   .   .

In the few years that I had been fighting regularly among the top-class of " light "-weight boxers, I had an average of thirty contests a year, with some of them coming in close succession. Twice, for instance, I had three bouts in a single week. I loved fighting : I had never found it difficult to be in trim, although some fights obviously needed stricter training than others, and I don't remember turning a fight down simply because I had no desire to go into the ring again.

Throughout the period, Ted Lewis, Johnny Basham, Jim Driscoll among the fighting section, and Peggy Bettinson, Callaghan, Corri, and countless others among the promoters and officials, had retained a belief in me that was surely enough in itself to put me on top of the world. Mentally I was there already. I think it was recognised throughout the boxing game in England that, for the time being, I could outlast any man within a stone of my weight, and there is something very satisfying about being in that position.

I just felt glad about it.

I had justified my own hopes and knew a large section of the boxing public was as pleased about it as I. I wonder if that public will ever know how much pleasure it gave me to feel that they were with me all the time ?

I am not trying to suggest that life was one long spell of perfect bliss. With the War getting more and more urgent, there was the constant desire to do something towards helping, even though I knew I would have some trouble in getting drafted overseas. Many people seemed to think I was pulling my weight by fighting, and yet more fighting, but it did not entirely satisfy me. There were the grumblers, with their pin-pricky accusations of cowardice ; threats of the white feather.

But I must confess that the coming contest with the Zulu Kid made me forget most things.

As usual I trained at home, where we were gradually introducing fresh livestock, and gaining new heart after the wipe-out in the storm. With me were five first-class sparring partners—Billy Fry, Jack Josephs, Gomer Evans, Dai Davies and George Jones. Every one of them deserves more than the honourable mention I am able to give them. They were all nine stone men, or more, and it was good to hear them say they would be glad when the Kid came over, and the fight was finished : they were more interested in ending a training period, I think, for I put all I knew into my sparring. Here, getting daily nearer, was a champion from another world, a man whose fame had reached us a while back ; an entirely different proposition, I believed, from anyone I had met before.

Oddly enough, the Zulu Kid gave me a new experience in the ring, but hardly the kind I expected.

Ted Lewis, as you will have gathered, was a man who rarely talked a lot. Ted's " yes," uttered with his head cocked down a little because of his increasing deafness, meant more than most men's long sentences. It was during my training for the Kid that Ted suffered sadly because of his handicap, and the rest of us received a lesson. I know we all suspected that the deafness was just a little exaggerated.

Ted came beaming into camp one day with an enormous parcel.

" Been shopping ? " someone called out.

" Eh—what's that ? "

" What have you been buying ? " someone bellowed close to his ear.

" Oh, one or two things," said Ted mildly, and then as an afterthought : " I've been to the barber."

He had been to the barber. And the barber had suggested a hair tonic : Ted, not hearing what the question was and anxious to please, had said " yes." Some special powder ? Yes, yes. A razor—yes, yes, Ted quite agreed. I think some of those patent preparations must still be in existence, and I knew the total bill came to nearly three pounds. It was typical of Ted that, rather than explain his affliction, he paid up bravely and carried his purchases away. I doubt whether he visited that barber again.

It is almost impossible to estimate the value of Ted's help, patience and advice, and it was the more remarkable that at the start he did it for nothing ! As a matter of fact, three of us had been fighting at Liverpool when the promoter came up.

" Isn't it time you boys looked after Mr. Lewis ? "

That puzzled us ; Percy Jones and Lew Edwards were with me, so I can only take a third of the blame.

" What way ? " asked one of us, and the promoter almost lost his temper.

" Lord love us, you fools, he does everything for you, and you give nothing to him. Nothing ! Get down to it right now and agree on a percentage of profits for him ! "

And we did.

But it took hours of argument to make Ted agree : he had no desire to make money out of us ; his one concern was for our success.

But to get to the Zulu Kid.

The fight was at the Holborn Stadium, just before Christmas, 1916, and it was packed to more than capacity. Ted had burst from his shell, and publicly declared :

> " Jimmy's condition and well-being are all that could be wished. The public have my assurance that the boy has finished his preparations in great shape and, providing nothing unforeseen happens in the meantime, he will enter the ring physically perfect."

The cautious Ted had to have that " providing nothing unforeseen."

I had felt cheerful—'Lisbeth called it chirpy—when we left Cardiff for London and the Holborn Stadium, and I found the Zulu Kid friendly enough at the weigh-in, where we had no difficulty in getting down to the weight. The American, a boy of Italian extraction, initiated something : his seconds tied a " Zulu " golliwog mascot to his corner. I was told that the golliwog gradually drooped and drooped, but I did not pay it a great deal of attention.

I mean no disparagement of a clever and plucky fighter such as the Zulu Kid proved himself in the eleven rounds that followed the first *ting !* of the gong, when I say that I was surprised at what happened. I sometimes wondered afterwards whether he was fit, although his supporters said that he was, both before and after. I do know that for the first time in the ring, towards the end of the eleventh round, I looked at the referee, hoping that he would stop the fight.

The Kid had taken as much punishment as I could give him. He had fallen, clutched at the rope, and pulled himself slowly to his feet, obviously dazed. A right to the chin shook him and actually made his

legs bend, so that he was standing and swaying helplessly, hands at his sides. But there was no stoppage,
and I had to finish the fight.

And so—the top of the world.

And, soon afterwards, the Army, where I was a
long way from the top of any world!

But there is a little sidelight on my training for
Zulu Kid that serves to show how easily preparations
can be upset. Our maid was taken ill in the night and
I knew she had to have a doctor. Hatless and coatless,
of course (I never realised my craziness about such
excursions until the damage was done), I hurried for
the doctor, and the rain hurried after me!

Ironically, I caught a cold and the maid's trouble
was only a passing colic. Luckily the cold soon passed,
accompanied by dire warning from Ted and others
that the Lee fight would not be the only one lost in
training if I could not find some sense.

Well, that was all right, but supposing I'd stayed
and the maid had died?

There was another sequel: the Kid had smashed
some heavy punches to the body and I went into a
nursing home under the care of that fine medical man,
Sir Herbert Barker. His treatment was little short of
miraculous.

Before joining the colours, Peggy Bettinson fixed
another open-air fight with the Bermondsey youngster,
Johnny Hughes. This time the weather was kind and
the sun did not shine too brightly. Neither of us
could complain that it was much different from indoor
fighting, except that to breathe fresh air was a strange
thing, and the crowd looked further away. This was
at Kensal Rise, and at the weigh-in there was some

argument, with not a little amusement, when Hughes was found to be a pound and a half over-weight. As I was considerably beneath it, I felt that it was justifiable to ask him to get the surplus off: in any case, Ted would have insisted. Johnny had to get rid of the excess there and then, while 'Lisbeth was waiting outside wondering what had caused the delay.

Hughes was an exceptionally powerful man for the weight, looking much heavier, with his thick-set shoulders and his fine, swarthy-looking arms and back. " Pocket Hercules " was a good nickname. He depended mostly on a swinging right, not difficult to avoid, which laid him open to the straight left more than was good for him. I used my feet more in that contest than usual, and had Hughes coming after me with those powerful swings, which hurt a lot when they did land. I kept jabbing his head back, and for the spectator it must have seemed on the dull side until Johnny swung a blow a trifle low. It was without intent I think, but enough to make me alter my tactics. I don't think he realised I had as much power left. In the tenth round, hardly recovered from a battering in round nine, he came at me with lowered head, had a warning, and then dropped his guard for my left feint for the stomach. My right came over for the finish.

'Lisbeth told me afterwards that a man leaned over and called her husband a miracle, a mite of a boy with a punch like that of a sledge-hammer. Well, people do talk like that, but the gentleman in question, an officer in a Scottish Regiment, turned out to be " Paddy " Slavin, who had been one of the heroes of the legendary battle at the N.S.C. twenty-four years before, when he fought and beat Peter Jackson. It was pleasant to think that he knew what he was talking about: so many don't, even when you meet them at the ringside, although the great majority are reliable, even expert. The safest guide is talk; the man who talks a lot often knows little.

And now I expect to be reminded that that is the case in other worlds besides boxing.

*

SANDHURST AND OTHER PLACES

SOON AFTER THE OPEN-AIR FIGHT IN WHICH PEGGY Bettinson proved himself a bad prophet by declaring he did not think there was a future in open-air fighting, I was able to enlist at last, only to be sent to Aldershot for training as an Instructor in the Army Physical Training Staff. On one occasion soon after I had been stationed there I had a motor-bike and a day off. Unfortunately I did not know a great deal about motor-cycles, but I wrote to 'Lisbeth, asking her to come down to Reading—on the Great Western line from Cardiff—where I would meet her. I knew she had not been well for a long time and I hoped it would cheer her up.

I did meet her, but fleetingly, and I don't know which of us was the more scared. I could not stop the bike, and careered round the station entrance until finally I had to make a dive for it, and get out on the road. A mile or so out the bike seized up. I pushed, pulled and cozened it, but had no luck, and when eventually I scraped into barracks on time I found a message waiting from 'Lisbeth. She telephoned shortly afterwards, too relieved that I was safe to be angry, and I was able to meet her next day—that time on foot.

It was just before being passed for the Army that Jack Johnson, the coloured heavy-weight and genial, friendly fellow, popular everywhere, asked me to take his part in a Revue, " Seconds Out." Jack had to go back to the States (he was an alien, of course) and he had to find someone if possible. But imagine me taking that giant's place! I hardly reached his waist.

I could not accept as it happened, but I would have enjoyed the first night, I fancy.

When I passed my certificate I was drafted to Sandhurst as Instructor. Here I was more or less on my own, although while training, Bombardier Billy Wells, Johnny Basham, Pat O'Keeffe, Ernie Barry and Jim Driscoll had been with me. Bombardier Billy is, as the world knows, one of the most good-natured men who ever put on the gloves, but some time afterwards we staged an exhibition fight, with the towering Billy and the midget " Tetrarch." Billy swiped, I ducked and ran and we had a glorious chase about the ring. Billy's gloves did not once touch me and afterwards I grinned at him.

" Tired, Billy ? "

" I'll tire you ! " said Billy, and without more ado he grabbed me, put me across his knee and proceeded in the accepted manner.

" Why don't you wear a glove ? " I asked him when I had wriggled free.

But a long time before that, Sandhurst. 'Lisbeth was able to take a small house near the college, and the authorities gave her every privilege. I think she enjoyed that period, with David—or " young Jimmy," and little Verdun. I was training as well as I could for a coming fight with Joe Conn, and I found two things to help me.

One was a Newport welter-weight named Charles —Young Charles, who had a gift for impersonation and was a screamingly funny auctioneer ! I often grew disgruntled during that period of training : I would have been lost without Charles and his fooling many a time.

My superior officer was also a boxing man, but with an unusual history. Captain John Hopley was a giant of six feet four and at Cambridge he had been persuaded to give up boxing in case he killed his man ! Hopley at the time I knew him weighed nearly sixteen stone : I was about six stone ten. With the possible exception of Ted Lewis, I have met no man with such an unfailing good temper, and he spared no effort to help me train.

Among the many distinguished people at Sandhurst was Prince Henry. He was tall and quite strong, but he did not particularly like boxing, in the ring, although he was a keen spectator. I remember he played a great deal of tennis and I also remember that Captain Hopley made sure we were on our toes when the Prince was in the gymnasium !

In May, 1918, I boxed an exhibition at Covent Garden with that old-time world bantam-weight champion, Pedlar Palmer. Pedlar was as old then as I am now, but he showed remarkable speed and cleverness that was sometimes dazzling. It brought the house down—and it was no ordinary house at the N.S.C. that night.

Jimmy White had hit on the happy idea of inviting a number of American soldiers and sailors as his guests to an exhibition and dinner. The N.S.C. warmly accepted the suggestion. Jimmy White made a pleasant little speech on the blood-brotherhood between England and America, and Sir F. E. Smith (later Lord Birkenhead) proposed the President and the American fighting forces. Admiral Sims and General Biddle, both at the ringside later, replied to the toast, followed by one to the American Press by Lord Burnham (then owner of the *Daily Telegraph*), and later Mr. (afterwards Sir) Walter de Frece proposed the Chairman. Jimmy White's reply was as witty and terse as usual. He was a practical joker out of the ordinary and always amusing, even just before his tragic death.

At the ringside, Peggy Bettinson made an unusually long speech for him (it lasted about four minutes) and I remember we had a thoroughly good show.

A long time afterwards Jimmy White "chairmanned" an entirely different "exhibition." He approached me one day on a delicate mission. At the Foxhill racing stables there was a larger-than-usual boy, useful with his fists and something of a bully. Jimmy believed that a hiding would knock sense into him, and asked me to join the stable.

Steve Donoghue was there, I remember, and all the guests knew the truth, but the stable lads had no idea. Sure enough our large one wanted to knock spots off me, and a ring-fight was fixed. I shall never forget the ludicrous expression on his face when I dodged, ducked, and landed him, always evading his whirling fists. I had to hit him once, of course! He was made to look thoroughly ridiculous, but he took it in good part and I believe Jimmy White had a laugh and made something of the boy. And it took me back in memory to the old booth days.

The official view of boxing after I was in the Army was, perhaps justifiably, disapproval of a contest for a purse, and there was trouble brewing when the fight with Conn was arranged for the Stamford Bridge Stadium in August, 1918. Jerry Cripps, the promoter, and Dan Sullivan and Dick Burge were worried in case the fight was forced off, but I kept training and grew more cheerful thanks to the united efforts of Young Charles, Idris Jones of Ammanford, a very good nine-stone boy, and Captain Hopley.

Jerry Cripps shouldered most of the anxieties of the preparations for the bout, and only he knew how nearly it did not materialise. Not only were the military authorities objecting, but the B.B.B.C. tried to stop it, as it was not under their auspices. Thanks in a large measure to the Rt. Hon. George Barnes (then in the War Cabinet) most of the difficulties were overcome, but to make sure that I was not detained at Sandhurst I sent off a decoy party with my wife and a second while I slipped into a train at Farnborough. I was not breaking regulations, for I had leave of absence. But I was not too happy about the prospects of climbing through the ropes.

Apart from the disciplinary rights and wrongs of the situation, there was the awkward fact that I ached to have the gloves on, and this was the first opportunity for some time in a serious contest. There was, also, the unfortunate fact that I could never properly get the hang of that discipline! I think this was chiefly due to the relaxation of the rules in the training corps and at Sandhurst, particularly with the Physical

Training Instructors. It had nothing at all to do with the fact that I was Jimmy Wilde. The Army is positively no respecter of persons, and you can find no one more capable than a cadet of shattering the illusions of fame. At a distance they can worship : at close quarters you have to walk right, sleep right, laugh right and talk right, with a dozen other qualifications ; and if you once break the rules of conduct—bang !

But they were good, keen fellows all of them, and they seemed to have only one objective : the battle-front. There were times when I envied them their opportunities, and there were others when I told myself not to be a fool. The War had lasted too long, by the time I went to Sandhurst, for anyone to imagine it was going to be a picnic : I wonder if a single soldier, after the first two years of conflict, really *ached* to get overseas—apart from the youngsters of the type I helped to train. They were certainly not irresponsible boys ; for their age, many of them were weighed down too heavily by a sense of responsibility, although they would break out in all manner of rags at odd times.

However, moralising is hardly a part of this story, so I shall get back to Joe Conn, the nine-stone London boxer, reckoned by many fine judges to be the best man at his weight in England, and a safe " bet " for world honours if he could get the chance of meeting the American champion. Conn was naturally super-confident. He had every reason to be, for he was getting the advantage of nearly two stone and for once my reach was going to give me no kind of advantage ; not even equality.

The outstanding contests for me, until then, had been the first bout with Sid Smith, at Liverpool, the unhappy affair with Tancy Lee at the N.S.C., the English Championship contest with Joe Symonds and the battle with the Zulu Kid. I do not necessarily mean that these fights had been the most difficult; they had loomed most important in the public eye, and *before* the fight they had all given me something different to think about, something bigger to overcome, or submit to. From the Conn fight onwards boxing led me on a very different trail. There were many ordinary fights, it is true, but more frequently really serious challengers were coming out. I was beginning to suffer for my reputation, finding proof enough that champions rose only to fall—if the other men had half a chance!

Probably I should not have been matched with a feather-weight but for the War; many of my friends, although they did not say so, believed I had taken on too much. Sullivan and Burge put £2,000 on Conn —big money in those days. I knew the difficulties and was practically certain of one thing : Conn would not be foolish enough to under-rate his opposition because of weight alone. How, then, could I beat the odds ?

Obviously I should have to change my tactics somewhat, and after considerable thought I decided it would be best to do a lot of missing. Had I breathed a word of this intention to anyone but 'Lisbeth, who, thanks be, had never criticised my tactics and was a safe recipient of every confidence, I should have been scoffed at. Anyhow, I entered the ring at Stamford Bridge with the firm intention to miss Conn frequently and to make him miss me as often.

By carving lumps out of the air I knew I should perhaps earn criticism from the ringside : as it happened, I did ! But nothing like so much energy is used up by a punch at the air as it is if the blow lands, particularly on a man of Conn's weight, who would not be likely to give way at all. I had to have time to size him up.

There were other things to be sized up, too, for the difficulties did not end with the boxing and military authorities. The police chose the day of the fight to come out on strike for the first time in a hundred years ! But Jerry Cripps was not daunted ; he arranged for some seven hundred men in light hospital blue to make a circle about the ring. They had come from various military hospitals, with the dual purpose of watching the fight and replacing the police.

So Conn and I passed the unusual men in blue and faced each other at last.

Conn, by the way, is one of the best-looking professional boxers I know, and I knew he was pretty clever from the first few rounds. We did the missing all right ! In fact, Conn kept on the defensive thoroughly, and though I was attacking I was not going for him as I might have done : I knew that if I did I might catch something entirely unexpected. That Conn was surprised by my tactics I could see— that sixth sense again !—but in round five he came to life.

He found my face with several heavy blows, and cut my lip severely. That gave him confidence, and he came in faster than before, re-opening a cut on my left eye. The damage made things look bad for my chances, and until round ten everything was going

Conn's way, but for one important fact that the crowd
could not see. Only one in five of his punches was
landing at all, and he was missing a lot. But I was
missing more, and that robbed Conn's miss-hits of
their importance. He was, I knew, tiring fast, and in
the tenth round I felt it safe to revert to normal
tactics, and I went at him. I assure you that I rarely
failed to connect after that, and Conn went down six
times in round ten, to have the fight stopped by the
referee two rounds later.

But I do not think I should have beaten Conn had
I gone for him early in the fight as I did later, although
I had expected—and said so after the fight—to win
earlier. Conn had a stronger defence than that of most
of the fighters I had so far met, and those early,
energy-sapping rounds had proved of vital importance.
I cannot hope to prove more conclusively the value of
ring-tactics, and by tactics I do not mean the simple
science of boxing. Boxing science does not admit
misses ; yet Conn lost because of them.

That victory did more to impress other boxers than
any fight I had yet taken part in, and I was glad.
Sid Smith said : " You can't beat him by fighting, and
you can't beat him by boxing, so what are you to
do ? " Pat O'Keeffe and the Birmingham boxer,
Owen Moran—a brilliant man with the gloves—were
equally generous, but I should like to give the statement of the referee after the fight. One has one's
pride !

Mr. J. T. Hulls said :

" Wilde is the mystery man of boxing. Conn
was neither over-trained, stage-struck nor lazy.

His downfall was brought about by Wilde's terrific punching. Before Jimmy finally cut loose he had stung Conn all over. I do not think there was any part of Conn's head or body that he did not visit before entering the tenth round.

" Conn certainly appeared to box in patches, and my excuse for him is that as soon as he carried the fight to his opponent that was Wilde's opportunity to punish him severely. . . .

" Some attribute the beginning of the end to a right-hand body punch in the tenth round but few noticed a hard uppercut he had received just previously. It landed under Conn's chin and I distinctly heard his teeth rattle.

" I still think that Conn, with Wilde out of the way, is the best man in England at nine stone."

I think I can safely agree with everything Hulls said : it is not always so easy to agree with the referee on every point ! But even the referee missed the significance of the " patchy " boxing.

The Hulls family is one that has devoted a great deal of time to boxing, for not only was J. T. a first-class referee, but his son Sydney is the renowned Harringay promoter of world-wide fame. Boxing is frequently hereditary, of course.

I think in some ways 'Lisbeth enjoyed the Chelsea fight as much as any, although she was worried about the authorities, who could be autocratic. However at the ringside she met Samuel Gompers, the shrewd Jewish-American Labour leader, Admiral Sims of the American Navy, who were equally keen fight fans, Mr. J. C. Gould, of whom more in a few moments,

and others who all helped to keep her mind off the
possibility of trouble.   I think she was afraid I should
be court-martialled !

It was unusual for 'Lisbeth to get separated from me
after a fight : we usually made the dressing-room
together.   However, we did get separated that day
and Mr. Gould went to collect 'Lisbeth.   Later we
went on to the Eccentric Club, that home of bachelors
presided over by Mr. Jerry Cripps.

There was a grand banquet to celebrate the victory
and 'Lisbeth was the only woman among a hundred
men.   But she was used to male company, though, to
make her comfortable, Mr. Gould said in the course of
a pleasant speech :

" And it's really good of Mr. Cripps and the
committee to have accorded Mrs. Wilde the honour
and privilege of dining in this room.   She is the only
woman to have done so."

'Lisbeth felt nearly as happy about that record as
about the earlier one at the N.S.C. !

With the fight over and the threat of military
interference apparently gone, we had to arrange the
purse somehow or other, for the authorities certainly
had to be convinced that no money was received by the
winner !   Mr. Bernard Oppenheimer had a grand idea.

A cup valued at a thousand pounds had been
suggested in the first place, but the new " get-out "
was to make 'Lisbeth a " present " of two packets of
diamonds, worth some £2000.   The Imperial Services
Boxing Association had sponsored the fight and raised
no objection to this unusual prize.   'Lisbeth received
those diamonds, the first time in her life she had such
jewellery : but *would* she keep them ?   Certainly not !

They were turned into cash as soon as possible, although the secrecy of the transaction was maintained and no trouble developed. I went back to Sandhurst and I don't think I was asked half a dozen questions about the fight. There is something in Army life to be really admired and the way everything is taken for granted is one of them.

There was one unhappy consequence of the Conn fight. Dan Sullivan and Dick Burge lost far more by backing Conn than they won in sponsoring the fight, and I believe they were both badly hit by their losses. Both recovered to play no small part in the boxing world. Burge's wife opened The Ring, Blackfriars, and among the men Sullivan has managed is Jack Doyle—who has promised (and at times achieved) so much, and who probably earned as much publicity as any fighter of his time.

I once nearly came a big cropper at the college. I had a telegram from the doctor at Tylorstown saying my wife was ill. It did not occur to me to get permission; I packed at once and took the first train to Wales, only to find two policemen waiting for me at home. The sergeant was a good fellow, however, and a talk with the doctor convinced him this was no ordinary desertion. A telegram to Sandhurst brought me news of two days' leave and again I escaped punishment for my sins. I had several rushed journeys to Tylorstown soon afterwards, for 'Lisbeth was seriously ill. The authorities could not have been more considerate and I began to wonder whether they had not deliberately turned a blind eye over the Conn bout.

Later, when 'Lisbeth was living nearby, our two-year-old Verdun cut his leg badly on a tin, and was rushed into the college hospital. 'Lisbeth frantically refused to let him be taken away by orderlies and nurses, but the surgeon reassured her, after a spirited protest, that she was not " a soldier to be ordered about ! " She was really frantic, for the boy was bleeding badly, and needed nine stitches ; now both father and son have leg scars.

That had happened a month or two before the Albert Hall hullabaloo.

I do not like sensations of any kind, but that was something out of the ordinary, and I remember being in an extremely bad temper afterwards, not because of the trouble but the reason for it. I had entered for the Inter-Allied Bantam-Weight Tournament at the Royal Albert Hall, to be held just a month after the declaration of the Armistice. Sir David Beatty (Admiral of the Fleet and afterwards Earl Beatty) was received on the first night with tremendous applause, but he was obviously far happier on his ship than as a speaker from the ring. He said briefly :

" This is not the time for speech-making. This is the time for fighting. I came here to see the finest exposition of boxing which can be produced by the Anglo-Saxon race. They say that the War is over and the talking begun. Therefore I had better get down."

That, after all, covered everything that was necessary, and the fact that it increased his popularity was, I'm sure, quite unintentional.

The contests were all for three rounds, and Pal Moore—officially C.P.O. Pal Moore, of the American

Army—was the most serious contender. Moore had a big name in the States, and by a two-to-one verdict he gained the decision that night. Although it would not be honest to say I was dazed, I had one of the shocks of my life when I heard that verdict. It had not occurred to me that Moore had been anywhere near winning.

I don't think the verdict could have been popular! The big crowd, somewhat worked up by the cessation of hostilities and all set for trouble, started it. There were representatives from every Colony and Dominion, and a goodly crowd of American sailors and soldiers, colloquially gobs and dough-boys.

King George V had arranged to come and give the prizes, but a cold kept him away and I remember feeling heartily glad. I was extremely sorry Prince Albert (our present King), who deputised, witnessed that demonstration. I had not liked the verdict, but this seemed too much of a protest. It looked like becoming a serious fracas, for the Americans were ready for a fight. It was Colonel Ronald Campbell (then director of the Army Physical Training) who found a way of stopping the riot—and it was a riot.

He sent for Driscoll—Regimental Sergeant-Major Driscoll then—and gave quick instructions. Jim jumped into the ring and I've never since seen him look so nervous, although only his friends realised that. 'Lisbeth once said: " He looked as upright as a pine tree, tanned and handsome and with his eyes flashing." Jim's eyes could flash, and the description fitted him well : he rivalled Conn for good looks.

The officers managed to get some kind of order

that lasted long enough for Jim to say—haltingly, let it be admitted :

" As trainer for the British team, I am satisfied with the decision." As simply as that.

Well, however unconvincing they sounded, the words worked. But it was one of the few occasions that I have known Jim tell a lie, even a white lie. He knew that the verdict had been a mistake : it was the incredibility of it that worried us, for there had not appeared to be anything even close in the three rounds. Pal Moore was not a hard hitter, and smacked a great deal with an open glove. Once he even grabbed my arm to stop me punching and I had to wait for the referee to break his hold !

It's strange that I still get worked up when I think of that bout. One of the aggravating pin-pricks afterwards was that Moore grew super-confident and was convinced he could beat me at any time, over any length. He told Eddie Kane that in so many words, and when he was offered a twenty-round contest he accepted it with :

" Sure I will, and I'll beat him again ! "

One way and the other it was an annoying business, and tempers grew frayed among the boys of my camp. By that time I was seeing the funny side of it, and it no longer proved even annoying.

There was some controversy in boxing circles, but to me the significant thing was that the Americans evidently did not think I was a worthy title-holder ; obviously they believed that the Zulu Kid victory had been a flash-in-the-pan. It incensed me at the time. I think I saw the incident somewhat out of proportion, but there was more than a three-round contest decision hanging fire.

I had signed for an American tour soon after being demobilised in 1919, and was half afraid it would be called off. Let me say in advance that, despite some odd adventures in the States, I found them grand people, and generous. Their methods are different from English methods, particularly with " ballyhoo," but when you get to know them they are as warm-hearted as you could wish. My experiences with American boxers, Pal Moore particularly, made me anxious to get busy over there.

My fear that I would not get the fight vanished when a cable from Mr. Walsh came asking " seventy-five hundred "—dollars, not pounds, it turned out—for a twenty-round contest, on Easter Monday. He asked the same terms to stage the fight in America.

Negotiations for the bout fell through, however, and it was some time before I met Moore again.

Joe Lynch, another name to conjure with, was in England early in 1919, and happily there was no trouble in arranging a contest at the N.S.C. In retrospect, it seems remarkable how the Club went on despite the fact that many familiar faces were missing, including Jerry Delaney, McCormick, the welter-weight, and Dai Roberts. The boxing world suffered as any other during the War. For some time it was almost melancholy to enter the doors, knowing who would not be there, and sad when one entered the ring, to see at the ringside scarred faces of men who had suffered badly.

Well, now for Joe Lynch.

The Irish-American had the reputation of being one

of the finest fighters America had ever produced. He had won a twelve-round contest with Pal Moore, and lost another—both on points—and his weight of eight and a half stone was well over a stone more than my own. The usual wavering among a section of the fighting world showed itself, although little of the rumours reached me in the wilds of my home training quarters. I was looking forward, in fact, to meeting any man from the States. I hated to think that America did not believe the Zulu Kid victory had been won on merits.

I had only partial satisfaction, however.

The verdict was for me, and I am sure that John H. Douglas, whose tragic death at sea with his cricketer-son, " J.W.H.T.," was one of the biggest blows to sport, knew exactly how the fight had gone, despite contrary opinions. But I had not at the time realised the big difference between the English and American methods of counting points. Later I will have an opportunity of showing you the way it affected me. The Americans were as puzzled (if that is the right word) as we were. It is one of the difficulties that will remain until there is an international agreement on the establishing of points verdicts. Unfortunately it does not look as though that agreement will come for some time yet.

I think the best way of describing the Lynch fight— which was another important milestone, and can certainly be added to the list of my important con-quests—is to give the opinion of a ringside critic who had watched me fighting dozens of times at the ring. I give this without prejudice :

" Jimmy beat Lynch. There is no question of

the decision in the minds of those who understand boxing. I know there was some dissent, and a few people went home in the belief that the American had been robbed of the decision, but such a thing is unthinkable. The referee's honesty and integrity were beyond question, and he is one of the greatest judges of boxing in the world.

" It was one of the most wonderful battles ever decided in the historic Club, and undoubtedly the greatest seen between the little men. It is my opinion that on the run of the fight Jimmy won on points, but I do say this : many sound judges of the sport are certain that Lynch could have won had he attacked as strongly as he could have. He seemed disinclined to risk being hit with one of Jimmy's mighty right-hand punches. And for this reason alone he deserved to lose. Lynch had two opportunities in the eighth and tenth rounds when he caught Jimmy with solid blows. But the champion understood his position, and like the wise old ring general he is, he did not let Lynch realise that the punches had shaken him.

" Eddie McGoorty, who was Lynch's principal advisor, kept shouting, to Lynch : ' Be careful of that right,' and Joe was extremely careful. I realise that the American party sincerely believed that Lynch had won well, yet they did not make any demonstration. They took their defeat like the good sportsmen they proved themselves to be.

" When you come to think of it, Jimmy's performance in lasting the fifteen rounds was astonishing. He was more than a stone the lighter man, and yet he compelled Lynch to box on a constant retreat for thirteen consecutive sessions. And the New Yorker in the ring was the recognised *bantam-weight* champion of the world.

" Lynch boxed throughout with such ultra-cautiousness that some of the spectators could not restrain themselves from the remark : ' Why don't you go in and have a fight ? ' This advice certainly seemed sound, but those who tendered it seemed to forget that Lynch could only fight on the lines which Jimmy allowed him to adopt. Jimmy exercised his brains the whole time like a chess-player. He made most of the winning moves : Lynch was generally in a crouching position. He tried every artifice to draw Jimmy into making a mistake, but he failed to disturb the little man's calmly calculated mind.

" From every point of view the fight was a classic from the first punch to the last, and the smart manœuvring of the pair was eloquent testimony that there were two thoroughbred fighters. Wilde's victory enhanced his reputation. He had, I have stated, won his most memorable match."

" Why didn't you open out, Joe ? " I was genuinely anxious to know, after the bout.

Lynch beamed all over his battered face.

" Well, I'm mighty pleased with what I've done," he said cheerfully. " McGoorty told me to keep away from you, and I think it was wise. Sure, I'm pleased to have stayed as long as I did with you."

After the fight I heard that J. H. Clifton had asked Joe why he did not go into Wilde ; Joe said :

" Well, it is easy to suggest going in and having a

fight, but Wilde is always dangerous, and besides he carries a knock-out punch in either hand at any period of a contest."

Funny how little things like that please one, isn't it? And here is another :

On the night of the contest, after I had gone upstairs to my bedroom at the N.S.C., there was a tap on the door ; and in walked the Prince of Wales, without any kind of preliminary announcement or warning. It is remarkable how some men can make themselves at home so quickly, without causing the slightest embarrassment. I have never known a moment's awkwardness with the Prince, and I have met him several times. On this occasion he shook hands, smiling.

" Good work, Jimmy, very well done. How do you feel ? "

" First rate," I assured him.

And he leaned against the dressing-table and chatted for a while, that persuasively friendly manner of his making me forget who he was. He had a genius for friendly *bonhomie* which is surely unrivalled.

Jim Driscoll was as certain as the rest of my supporters that the verdict had been right. With easy smile and perpetual cheerfulness, Jim was one of the most reliable men with me. I remember that he taught me the vital necessity of the straight left, which Dai Davies had always rubbed in, by the simple expedient of using it when we were sparring. He preferred sparring with better-class fighters, and he would grin as he landed punch after punch on my nose or chin.

" See, Jimmy, that's the way—like that—that— that ! "

It did two things, in the earlier days of my championship boxing. It helped me to counter the left jab, and taught me its own effectiveness as an attacking punch, for those blows stung. I had always relied on my right, from which most of my knock-outs were to come. But the straight left so often paved the way that it is difficult to say which was the more important punch. To the beginner, let me say without hesitation, the straight left. Everyone *can* be trained to use that punch effectively, while the right punch, if not entirely natural, is one that certain boxers can develop more effectively than others. Some of the best boxers of my acquaintance just cannot use it really effectively, and smaller men seem to have it more frequently than the heavier weights.

Jim Driscoll was always welcome at Tylorstown, but he nearly caused trouble on one occasion. I am going back a little now to the time when we had appeared in the same ring in Sheffield—promoted by the late Mr. Billy Widdison. I have a gold and platinum watch-chain which Billy gave me. His generosity was well known.

Until that time, and for a long time afterwards, I had always caught a train home on the night after the fight. Jim had different habits, chiefly because he was a great racing fan ; when he was near a course he had to stay for the races. He persuaded me—and anyone who knew him knew how easily he could convince one of the sterling motives of his suggestions—and I fell.

We were away three days and I learned a lot about racing at Doncaster. He made sure we had a glorious time.

After leaving Jim, however, I developed cold feet. 'Lisbeth would not readily accept an explanation, and the brief wire I sent on the third day merely told her

that I should have written before. I had no alibi. Jim
had a way out and recommended it before leaving me.

" Buy her something, Jimmy, that'll do the trick."

" Well, buy what ? " I asked. (Yes, I was as
innocent as that !)

We decided on a pink silk blouse, and in those days
blouses of silk were something out of the ordinary.

When 'Lisbeth got it and understood my motive
for sending it, she promptly put it on the fire, afterwards telling me with great emphasis that she enjoyed
seeing it burn. A peace-offering indeed !

Somewhat worried despite the offering, I decided
to call on other counsellors than Driscoll, and asked
'Lisbeth's mother what she could recommend.

" Go round and throw your hat through the
window," she said promptly. " If 'Lisbeth's really
angry she'll throw it out again, and you want to wait
a bit. If she keeps it in——"

Well, she kept it in. She also told me what she
thought of Jim, blouse, bribery and corruption, and
husbands. With bowed head I waited for the storm
to pass, tentatively suggesting that she should blame
Jim. That worked.

The next milestone in my fighting life, after the Lynch
contest, was in July, 1919, and it was a fight that I
had hankered after for months : that return slam with
the American, Pal Moore. C. B. Cochran promoted
it at Olympia, with the largest purse I had ever then
fought for : £5,000, three for the winner and two
for the loser, and a side-stake of £1,000. Before
and during the War the biggest purse had been £2,000.
It gave a vivid illustration of the change of values.

C. B. Cochran promoted several of my bigger

fights, and was a man to be thoroughly relied on to make things hum. As he mentioned, during a recent broadcast, he has done many things besides finding young ladies, and he must have lost and won hundreds of thousands in promoting big fights. Who can fail to remember the Carpentier-Beckett fiasco at the Holborn Stadium in December, 1919, when people paid five guineas to stand and watch seventy-five seconds of fighting ?

I shall always treasure a remark made by the inimitable " Cocky," when I met him casually after the 1927 fight between Micky Walker and Tommy Milligan. The suicide of Jimmy White, of whom more later, had robbed the fight of its publicity and Cochran lost some £15,000.

" Do you know, Jimmy," he told me, " you and Carpentier are the only two men who have ever earned me money in boxing."

When C. B. heard of the book, he sent me the following letter :

12th August, 1938.

One of the greatest difficulties of the play producer, having found a play, is to cast it to his entire satisfaction. Strangely enough the same difficulty presents itself to the boxing promoter. In the years when I was most active in boxing promotion I had a good choice of heavy-weights ; there were Joe Beckett, Bombardier Billy Wells, Frank Goddard, Dick Smith and Jack Curphey, with Corporal J. Blumenfeld (later Jack Bloomfield) just coming along.

For big gates, with one exception, I had to put up heavy-weight matches. The exception was Jimmy Wilde, but here the casting difficulty set in.

Where were the opponents to come from? Jimmy Wilde was in a class by himself. That was his tragedy. When he fought he was nearly always giving weight away. Even when he boxed Pal Moore for me at Olympia he was about 7 stone 4 lb. to Moore's 8 stone 4 lb.

This was a great match and gave me as much pleasure as any of my promotions. I look back with pride to that great night in July, 1919, when my old friend, Eugene Corri, gave the decision to Jimmy after a terrific twenty rounds.

One of the greatest moments of Jimmy Wilde's career must have been that last round (the twentieth) when he scored with left and right, and in the last couple of seconds came near knocking Moore out. I was sitting between the Prince of Wales and General Pershing. Both asked me to convey congratulations to our Jimmy.

My career has brought me in touch with all kinds of people, but with no finer little sportsman than Jimmy Wilde, and if his body had been in proportion to the size of his heart we should have had and held for several years the heavy-weight boxing championship of the world.

At any important boxing match in England to-day Jimmy Wilde is almost as great an object of interest as the principals in the ring.

During my recent long stay in the United States wherever I mixed in boxing circles from coast to coast there were enquiries about Jimmy, and expressions of admiration. Jimmy Wilde is a great national institution. Long life to him and great success to his book.   CHARLES B. COCHRAN.

CHAPTER X

★

"'WISP OF A BOY!'"

PUBLIC INTEREST IN THE CONTEST WITH PAL MOORE was the greater because of the decision against me in our three-round fight, which aroused the storm of controversy. I have been the subject of many wordy battles, but none of my fights had caused anything like the bitterness the Albert Hall decision had done. Sometimes I felt sorry for the military judges who had roused the storm, but never so sorry as for Jim Driscoll, who still remembered that unpleasant job of pouring oil on the troubled waters, and frequently said it was the worst moment he ever suffered from military discipline.

I had no illusions about Moore.

He was strong, and he could fight, while he was perhaps the most confident boxer I was likely to meet in the ring for a long time to come. It was odd to see the Stars and Stripes hanging and fluttering in his corner, pleasant to hear the reception that Moore received from the crowd. There was to be no prejudice, at all events. It is surprising how I reacted more to a demonstration against the other man than a little show against me—and in America I found them sometimes. They did not worry me at all. I think it was the consciousness with which I determined to

let nothing rile me and to make sure my detachment in
the ring was all that it should be. But the determination proved an armour-plating with holes when the
disturbance started about the other man. Sometimes
I wonder what would have happened had opposing
camps realised it before the fights : would there
have been a show of organised hostility against my
opponent ?

Moore was an unusual fighter : a type I had not met
a great deal before. We called him a flapper—no
relation to the forerunners of the Bright Young
Things—because he did not punch with his knuckles.

I was not to discover the importance of that until
later.

How that straight left, dinned into me by Driscoll,
came in useful during the twenty rounds with Pal
Moore—the straight left, footwork and an occasional
right when he left himself open. A man fighting as
fiercely as Moore had to leave himself open at times,
but he could take all the punishment going. That
superabundant confidence of his stood him in fine
stead.

Something almost unique in my contests happened
at the end of the ninth round. I had punched his
ears sharply just before the gong went : Moore's
head was ringing, and he did not hear the gong. As
I dropped my arms, he came at me like a tiger, and I
took more punishment than I wanted. It was a clear
case of a misunderstanding, and I was glad—despite
yells from the crowd—that Corri did not disqualify
him. (That was the occasion of the whispered apology
from Corri, because General Pershing, as well as the
Prince of Wales, was present.) The crowd yelled for

blood again when Moore's open glove kept flicking the back of my neck. To be honest, I objected myself. In many ways Moore's ideas of boxing and my own were entirely different : there can hardly have been more widely contrasting exponents of the fight game in the world.

In the fourteenth round I took a breather. Moore, smiling and obviously confident that he had tired me, caught me a fierce blow on the chin, cutting my lip and drawing blood. Consequently, in the fifteenth I sailed right into him, and I think he had a shock. I certainly did when, rushing at me with his head down, his skull caught the bridge of my nose ; damaging it more than any fist had ever done !

I remember shouting to Corri : " It's all right, it's all right ! " And I yelled at Moore : " Come on, then, come on ! " He did, and the last rounds were as fast as any of the fight. I had never been nearer to losing my temper.

I don't think there was any doubt of the justice of the decision, and I know that Corri had no hesitation in pointing to me. But the Moore corner protested vigorously : certainly Pal had put up a tremendous fight, and when I learned more about his training and general boxing methods (I am talking of the American school, not Moore in particular) it was easier to understand the protest. Perhaps you will better understand my own confidence in the correctness of the verdict when I say that I did not remember him getting home one clean punch with a *closed* glove. He did not try to, because points were counted in the States for the " flap " hit, which is disregarded in England and for which boxers are warned.

The verdict was warmly received, and I felt satisfied.

My next fight is of more interest because of an " accident " to Peggy Bettinson. It was at the West London Stadium, a picture-house which he had leased during the War. There was only a small seating capacity and for the half-crown seats a queue over a quarter of a mile long lined up. The rush proved more than the usual staff could tackle. Peggy arranged with Jimmy Lambert, now Inspector of the British Boxing Board of Control, to look after the box office in the gallery.

It was hard to imagine gruff and rare-speaking Peggy Bettinson in that box, and I can wager he wished he had not gone in !

Here is Lambert's description :

" It was a cubby hole with a gas flare and the ceiling barely five feet from the ground. Into this little cupboard the Governor pushed his big frame. But he had to keep his head bent, and every time he raised it, he bumped against the ceiling. He was kept busy there for two hours, until the gallery was jammed to capacity. Peggy must have suffered all the torments imaginable, and he was not the smoothest-tempered man I have known !

" When at last he came out his head was still bent and he could not raise it. He was in considerable pain, perspiration rolled down his face— and he was to referee the contest ! "

I can vouch for the fact that he refereed it well !

As Peggy Bettinson loomed as large in my boxing life as any man except those constantly with me, it is understandable that I was always anxious to give my

services for his benefit nights : but so were all the
first-class boxers. So the N.S.C. was always inundated
with offers for these nights, from fighters who often
withstood tempting offers from promoters, but were
prepared to box for Bettinson without getting a
penny. I hardly think Peggy ever had a poor benefit,
and if any man deserved to do well he did.

Two other unusual things happened in the West
London Stadium fight which was with an old
opponent, Sam Keller. In the first place Sam could
not make the weight : he was a pound and a half
over eight stone three pounds and Ted Lewis was
angry about it. Ted so rarely lost his temper that it
was an event. He wanted to call the fight off, but was
satisfied with the £10 forfeit, after it had been pointed
out that the crowd would be disappointed, and many
Welshmen had travelled down. Ted would do anything rather than feel he had broken a moral " contract " with the public.

The other thing, just to show the absurd contrasts
in the boxing game, was that 'Lisbeth sat at the ring
next to a distinguished-looking man who, after the
fight, I learned was H. B. Irving. 'Lisbeth told me he
took a keen and knowledgeable interest in the boxing,
and was hungry for information about me. I glowed
in that reflected glory, and wished I had met him.

Kellar retired in the eighth round : I always
preferred a man to retire than take tremendous
punishment for the privilege of being knocked out.
Miracles do happen in the ring, but usually if a man is
being badly battered he has little chance of pulling
through. To me, at least, it was always obvious when
an opponent stood no chance : I often wished they

lacked some of the courage that kept them on their feet.

A case in point was my fight with the American, Young Rosner. This was at the Liverpool Stadium soon afterwards, and it was freely asserted afterwards that Rosner was temporarily blinded early in the fight. This was not altogether true. He had received a scalp wound during training (naturally I knew nothing of that until afterwards) and one of my early punches re-opened it. I also re-opened old wounds above both eyes, and that fight was one of the goriest I have ever taken part in. Blood simply streamed from the wounds and, at the start at least, gave a wrong impression of Rosner's condition : he was nothing like as bad as he looked.

He proved it in the ring.

He was fast, his footwork was excellent, and he had one trick worth a great deal. He would " cover up," completely hiding his head, and bending, then uncoil himself and let fly with his right. It was never possible to be sure when the blow would come, and he landed several heavy punches. Once or twice he was cautioned for hitting low, but I am sure he did it accidentally. There were moments when he could not see because of the blood, and whenever I landed there was " paint-mark " on him.

It was during the fifth round that the first low blow came, and fast upon it Rosner's :

" Sorry, Jimmy ! That sure was an accident ! "

It takes something to find time for an apology when you are being welted badly. But perhaps the most remarkable thing about Rosner during that fight was that *he never once retreated*. Nothing else could have shown his spirit so well, although tactically I think he was mistaken. I have never been more certain that seconds were wrong, for Rosner was, after all, in danger of losing his sight, and the fight should have been stopped a long way before the eleventh round. I think Eugene Corri felt the same, for he was very tolerant of those low blows, which might have caused a lot of damage had they landed with any power.

During 1919 I went over to Paris to box in a fête promoted for the French refugees, and during the show fought an exhibition with Georges Carpentier, who had already gained something of a reputation both for boxing and for charm. Nothing of the newspaper reports of Georges' charm and scintillating personality has been exaggerated. He was (and is) an astonishing fellow in many ways.

I remember his wife, a charming woman herself, coming to me after the bout.

" You are a bad man, M'sieu Wilde. You are so fast, yes, you make my 'usband fight too hard, sweat too much."

" It will do me good," protested Georges.

" Oh, no. I know what is good for you ! " Madame Carpentier assured him, and the last word went to her.

There must have been ten thousand people at the fête, and the cheering lasted for many minutes. In England, America and Paris I have heard more applause for an exhibition bout than for a real fight, which seems to me a sure indication that most people interested in boxing prefer boxing to fighting, and to sheer brute strength.

It was in the evening that I went out with Georges,

Photo: Central News

SERGEANT INSTRUCTOR JIMMY WILDE AND
MRS. WILDE, 1918

THE JOE CONN FIGHT IN 1918, WHEN THE
PURSE WAS PAID IN DIAMONDS

THE PAL MOORE FIGHT
Top right shows a typical Moore 'flap hit'.

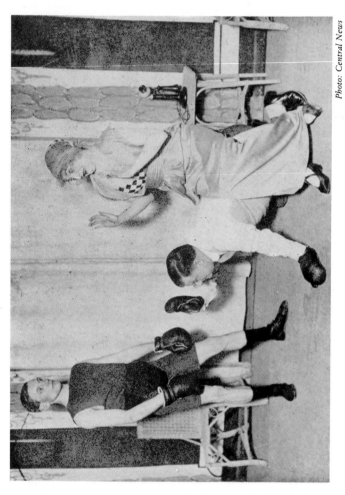

IN THE REVUE, *HALF-PAST EIGHT*

ON HIS CHICKEN FARM ON THE SLOPES OF
PENRHYS

Every bird and animal, except one dog, perished in a snow-storm in which Jimmy Wilde's father-in-law nearly lost his life.

MR. & MRS. JIMMY WILDE AND THEIR TWO SONS, DAVID
(TALLER) AND VERDUN, WITH FRIENDS AT NEW JERSEY,
IN 1928

With the kind permission of Tom Webster

Photo: Central News

A RECENT PHOTOGRAPH, JIMMY WILDE (*On top*) AND (*Left to right*): LOUIE BOTESS, DAVID WILDE, JACKIE PHILLIPS, TED PHILLIPS AND EDDIE M'QUIRE

his wife, Tom Webster and one or two other friends. I wish, by the way, that a boxer's life could last as long as a cartoonist's! Tom Webster's incomparable sporting cartoons seem to get better all the time: but he is a humorist two ways, and that night he chose me as his foil. I didn't know him as well then as I do now, and when he assured me that the wine was innocuous, I believed him, breaking my rule of one glass at a time—the times few and far between.

Luckily the two glasses did not make me feel war-like. I remember little about it, but I know they had to take me home and put me to bed, while I had a head like a kicking horse next morning. And if you ask Tom about the "quickest drunk" he's ever seen, you'll hear the story in a far more effective fashion than I can recount it!

It was after this that I had a rare experience.

I met a fighter nearly half a stone lighter than myself and for the first time in my life I towered above an opponent. The fight was one of the funniest I have ever been in. The little wisp of a boy—he was no more—was the Frenchman, Husson, and the fight lasted for seven rounds. I had some idea during it what my bigger opponents thought of me, for that Frenchman was a positive will-o'-the-wisp. He had obviously made up his mind not to let me hit him, and I was chasing him all round the ring, to try and get a telling punch. I did manage to get him in a corner once, and lead several times to the body—one, a trifle low, calling for a "more careful with your punches, Wilde!" from Referee John Angle.

Now and again Husson would stop dancing back, and flash a hopeful blow toward me, and then off

again for the dance. I was glad when a stomach-
blow finally winded him and he was counted out,
gasping for breath. I had hated the idea of hitting
him on the chin : he was absurdly small—so small that
once a stentorian voice once yelled out :

" I'll fetch you a butterfly-net, Jimmy ! "

Believe me, I could have done with one for Husson.

I was still smiling when I reached the hotel. A wag
had left a decorated walking-stick and a pair of bright
yellow gloves for me, and I wore them as I walked in.

Immediately a complete stranger jumped across the
hall, gripped my hand and pumped it up and down.

" It's an honour to meet you, sir, an honour to
meet you ! "

I said how nice it was of him to say so, but was
completely lost by a spate of talk that went miles
above my head. Finally he said something I could
understand, if only in part.

" To be the brother of such a man, sir, it is a
privilege beyond words. Such genius, such——"
and a great deal more like that. Then came the
revelation :

" When I read the wonderful *Picture of Dorian Grey*,
Mr. Wilde, I realised the illimitable heights to which
a genius could ascend. I——"

Of course, I had to disillusion him : he had taken
me for the brother of Oscar Wilde ! Probably my
yellow gloves had played their part in helping me to
look like the brother of a genius of literature.

By then it was getting increasingly obvious that
we should have to make the trip to the States. After
the Pal Moore fight, cables were constantly arriving,
and I think I was offered fights at most of the big

towns in America. I was anxious to go but had to make sure such a trip would be a financial success. Finally Ted Lewis accepted an offer to fight Jack Sharkey, the New York bantam, reputed to be far better than me. The Milwaukee Auditorium was to be the scene of the contest and the terms were good.

Ted Lewis was down in the mouth about the trip.

"I can't leave my business, Jimmy, but I hate to think of you going alone."

"I wish you could have come," I told him, and I have never been more sincere. "But I've got to take it now, Ted." Ted agreed but I know he was miserable at staying behind.

CHAPTER XI

★

AMERICA

AT LAST WE LEFT FOR THE STATES. I REMEMBER THE excitement of the preparations and the high hopes we held of the tour. 'Lisbeth was with me. David Hughes came over as manager and Benny Williams was trainer.

Benny had been with me a great deal. He had met Ted Lewis through their mutual interest in the race-track, Ted as starter, Benny, for many years, as a first-class runner in anything from the hundred yards to the half-mile. There was not much that Benny did not know about training, much to my advantage.

My chief recollections of the voyage (on the *Baltic*) is of wishing I had never been born. The sea was dreadful, and we were hardly out of Southampton than the waves began to look like the Welsh Mountains gone mobile. My only consolation was that I was one of the hundreds to feel as bad, and after the first day I was in the sick-berth most of the time. So was David Hughes and Benny, but not 'Lisbeth; oh no, not 'Lisbeth!

She had never been on a long sea-trip before, and it is hard to understand why she was not affected. I was told afterwards that the only other passenger who managed to make the whole crossing without trouble was a huge Canadian rancher.

It is no exaggeration to say that he was bigger than Primo Carnera, and to picture him walking the decks with 'Lisbeth, who is hardly as tall as me, must have afforded the crew some high moments. Apparently our rancher friend was constantly yearning to emulate me. There were lots of people he badly wanted to punch.

We reached Halifax after the liner had been posted as missing, to find we were forced to stay there for six hours. 'Lisbeth went off to look at the shops while I walked gratefully to dry land ; and she came back soon afterwards, as excited as I have ever seen her, with a complete stranger.

" Jimmy, this is Mrs. Roberts from—you would never guess—Tylorstown ! "

Yes, it's a small world. Mrs. Roberts had recognised 'Lisbeth from photographs, and introduced herself. She insisted on us crowding into her small flat for tea and her Canadian husband, whom she had married during the War, burst out from time to time :

" Gee—can you believe it ! "

It was certainly difficult to believe that we should meet someone from Tylorstown the first day ashore, and one whom I had known as a little girl.

We left soon afterwards for New York, after saying good-bye to our new-found friends on the quay. It seems absurd for me to make any comments on that wonderful New York sky-line. It is more stupendous now than it was then, but it was a thing of wonder, with its incredibly high buildings. It was like a fantasy : majestic, wonderful.

Another thing of wonder was the crowd.

The police, I learned, had to draw their batons to keep them from breaking down the rails to get a glimpse of the much-heralded " Mighty Atom." Here was my first real taste of the effects of American publicity methods, and I must admit that I felt warmed when I realised the reception was for me.

But there will always be contrasts.

The contrast came after we had met the promoters and arranged the contract for the fight at Milwaukee, fixing the match provisionally for December 6th. On the previous night a banquet had been given in our honour, and I think I should have enjoyed it more if I had had longer to get over the effect of that rough crossing. But I appreciated it enormously.

Then came the task of finding quarters.

'Lisbeth, quite rightly, would not stay at an hotel, and we went to an estate agent's in search of a flat. I have never known rain like we had that day. It seemed to drop from the skies, unceasing, noisy, almost drowning us. We were finally recommended to a flat in New Jersey. This was towards evening, and it took us some time to find the place, but satisfied at last, and hopeful of being able to settle in immediately, imagine our horror at finding the door closed against us after the maid had taken our names ! We were left on the doorstep, with the rain driving in and none of us able to find a word.

Worse was to follow.

Boxers were not popular with the owner of the flat, and she did not want us to have it. But that time we would have been prepared to offer anything in the way of rent, and finally she agreed to let us take over in three days' time.

" But can't we stay for the night ? " David Hughes asked pleadingly. " It's nearly midnight, there are not many hotels empty, we——"

" In three days' time ! " said the landlady vehemently, and out we went into the rain. I remember wishing Jim Driscoll, with his Irish charm, could have been there to help us.

'Lisbeth had positively refused to leave the matter entirely to agents, and I think perhaps she wished for once that she had agreed to let someone else find our quarters. Her determination was chiefly due to the need for finding a quiet place, where she could do all the necessary cooking. I was to be made to feel at home in every way—we had even brought a good supply of tea, so that we could make it English fashion.

Finally, after calling at hotel after hotel, we found a little place where they had to rig up a temporary kitchen for us, ready to give us shelter. But that tramp through the torrential rain is a thing to remember : who cared if I were the World Champion ?

I know my many American friends will understand me when I say that the contrasts in America were bewildering. One night fêted and banquetted, a milling crowd at the docks to welcome us : the next tramping—all four of us—through the rain of New Jersey looking for an hotel, and begging unsuccessfully for shelter !

Flats were difficult to get, and we had to accept our landlady's word that we could move in in three days. She kept it—I think that woman was one of the most downright I have ever met—and with sighs of relief we settled in.

I think 'Lisbeth was right to do the cooking, for a change of diet, with the American food (so different in many ways from ours) might have caused serious trouble. But I fancy our preference for being on our

own was a little misunderstood : I have never liked
" ballyhoo " too much ; the comforts of home life
have always attracted me, perhaps because I knew so
little of real comfort in the early days. Consequently
the newspapermen and others gathered an impression
that we were too aloof : it did not help our reputation,
even if it was easily understandable. As a matter of
fact I was not aware that anything was the matter for
a long time.

Our English tea certainly made us popular with
others from home. Heavy-weight Jack Bloomfield
was frequently in and out of the " camp," while
T. O. Williams, from Cardiff, had been buying timber
for pit-props in Labrador and travelled all the way to
New Jersey to see me fight. He also appreciated the
rarity of our tea.

We played a great deal of bridge in the evenings,
and were lucky in finding several neighbours equally
enthusiastic, and very friendly. 'Lisbeth had all the
luck in the world : I have never known her hold so
many aces, but we were puzzled one evening when
someone said in tones of disgust :

" You must have seen the barber, Mrs. Wilde."

" Indeed I haven't ! " retorted 'Lisbeth, who has
always worn her hair long ; and there was a gust of
laughter. The barber in question was a noted local
bridge-fiend, who had similar luck with the cards.

A few evenings later we were playing against
different opponents and 'Lisbeth in turn looked at a
man who had taken her luck with a vengeance.

" You must have seen the barber," she told him
cheerfully. " I——"

And then we were frozen by the expression on the

man's face. He *was* the barber, and touchy about his reputation for holding aces !

I had not been in the States long before I had a shock.

We had all taken it for granted that the arrangements for the Sharkey fight were as good as a contract, but there were many formalities to go through, although I think the promoter, Mr. Otto Borchert had an idea that some of the difficulties could be avoided. By the rules of the International Sporting Club I had to appear before them *prior to* fighting in the more profitable States. It transpired that they could not fix a fight for me before February 1st—three months ahead !—while trouble with the building of their arena made it more likely March 1st.

We were more than thankful to the Club for making so many exceptions for me, while Mr. Tex Rickard was very friendly and helpful. I remember, at the Biltmore Hotel, when we went to dinner, he said laughingly :

" I can't make you out, Jimmy. You're just a bag of bones."

" He is," said 'Lisbeth.

Tex laughed.

" And to see him smiling to himself like a schoolboy, it's startling. I only wish I could get a New York licence for him."

With his help, and the co-operation of the Club, it was arranged that I should fight anywhere but in New York State. Otto Borchert came along with the contract which gave rise to considerable arguments and made trouble for me with the Press. Here is the agreement :

MEMORANDUM OF AGREEMENT

THIS AGREEMENT, made and entered this 20th day of November, A.D. 1919, by and between JIMMY WILDE, of the City of London, Country of England, party of the first part, and JACK SHARKEY, of New York City, New York,

WITNESSETH:

That the second party hereby agrees to enter into a boxing contest before the Cream City Athletic Club of Milwaukee, Wis., a corporation duly organized under the laws of the State of Wisconsin, on the night of December 6th, 1919, at The Auditorium under the management of Otto Borchert, President of the Club.

It is agreed that Jack Sharkey, of New York, party of the second part, will weigh in, in private, before Jimmy Wilde and representatives of both parties, at not more than 116 pounds weight at 7 o'clock P.M. on the night of the contest, namely, the 6th day of December, 1919.

Party of the second part shall deposit the sum of Two Thousand dollars ($2,000.00) with some person agreed upon by Jimmy Wilde, party of the first part, and it is further understood that in the event of Jack Sharkey, party of the second part, weighing more than 116 pounds at 7 o'clock P.M. on the day of the contest, he shall forfeit the Two thousand dollars ($2,000.00) to Jimmy Wilde, party of the first part.

It is further understood that this agreement shall be binding and without recourse to law.

Witnesses:

Otto Borchert

George Lawrence

Jack Sharkey

Jimmy H. Wilde

The trouble was over weights, not money, as it was generally believed. My best fighting weight was 100 pounds, and I naturally wanted to get down to it. Sharkey would come no lower than 118 pounds, and by the Wisconsin State Rules, a boxer could only give away 10 pounds. Finally he conceded that the weigh-in should be at seven o'clock. The fight was at nine-thirty and thus I would have two and a half hours to get down to normal, after making as much weight as I could for the weigh-in. I did not want to accept this, but it meant no fight unless I gave way, and I must admit that I did so unhappily.

We prepared immediately to travel to Milwaukee, anxious to be getting into serious trim. The delays, arguments and technical difficulties were worrying, but none of our party looked backwards ; things were settled.

We were actually preparing to bundle into a taxi when a cable came, to cause the biggest excitement during the trip.

The Prince of Wales (remember this was 1919) was in New York Harbour, on H.M.S. *Renown,* and he asked us to visit him. Milwaukee, Sharkey, tickets and taxis could go to perdition : we were going to the *Renown !*

The Prince greeted us warmly. Tea, English fashion, was very pleasant, and 'Lisbeth produced her autograph-book.

" Of course," said the Prince, and signed it. " Are you going to have a successful tour, Jimmy ? "

" Well, I think so."

" You ought to," he assured me. " I wish I could stay for the Sharkey match, but I must get back.

I'll leave you to show America what you can do."

Before we left he showed us over the *Renown*, chatting in the friendliest fashion, and laughingly declaring that it was his first chance of entertaining me, instead of letting me do the entertaining.

But that red letter afternoon had to finish, although as we shook hands he said again, a little wistfully, I thought, that he wished he could stay for the first match.

We missed our train but it was not a serious delay. In America the Prince would have been forgiven for anything, anyhow. It was bitterly cold when we reached Milwaukee, and the others suffered from frostbite, but I was lucky in avoiding anything serious.

I had many varying impressions when at last we settled in Milwaukee. I had already discovered that training was done at public gymnasia, where a fee was charged for the public to see the contestants going through the mill. An excellent idea, and one that I think could be developed to advantage in this country. One can always be reasonably sure of finding adequate training quarters in the States.

Against this, however, was the fact that houses were almost impossible to find. We had always been used to training at home, and it had become a fetish for 'Lisbeth to do the cooking. That brawn which had caused ptomaine poisoning was always held up as a horrific example of the results of eating ready-cooked food! Looking for a flat in New York had been easy compared with looking for a house in Milwaukee, but finally we found one at Wauwatosa, some five miles from the city.

The search had interfered with training, but at last I was able to get going. The Milwaukee Athletic Club, after inviting me to a luncheon, asked me to train at their gymnasium, a signal honour for a visiting fighter: everywhere I was made to feel at home despite a wave of anti-English feeling current just then because of the Irish trouble.

Before starting in earnest, by the way, I had to see Mr. Walter Liginger, chairman of the Wisconsin Boxing Commission, whose rules are as strict as any I have encountered.

For instance, you must reside in the State three days before a fight, and, before the contest, must give a three-round exhibition to prove you are a fit person to appear in the ring. There are anomalies caused by this, and I could not help but feel in many ways the precautions were overdone.

I found Mr. Liginger a charming personality, however, and he certainly interpreted the rules in a way to prevent them from irritating.

Promoter Otto Borchert had been equally pleasant all through, but I was disappointed when he asked me to train for a week in Chicago: I have always disliked travelling while training. However, as he was set on it and had done so much to make our first weeks pleasant, I could not refuse. Chicago, when I first saw it, was yellow and foggy. It was not unlike London—I wonder if that comparison has ever been made before?—although I was conscious of no nostalgia for home.

Nothing went wrong on the journeys to and from Chicago, but I was glad to get back at Milwaukee. I had not fought for a long time, and I felt stiff and awkward, while I sparred mostly with Al Thompson, who was more than twenty pounds above my weight. That did not help me to get sprightly. But the severest jolt came when I discovered Jack Sharkey at the same gymnasium! That was an unheard of situation in England, but the accepted thing in the States. I think it is better avoided, but that is probably the prejudice of my own customs.

The warmth of my welcome in Milwaukee is a thing that I shall never forget, despite the unhappiness we suffered afterwards. When I went to the Auditorium—a vast, pillarless stadium, almost fantastic—to see the Dundee-White bout, the sport fans would not leave me alone. I was introduced from the ring, thus creating a precedent.

Nowadays we are beginning to learn how insignificant records are, but there is still considerable pleasure from making them.

I was induced to make a speech. Far more courageous, I think, was the crowd's pretence at liking it : no one will ever call me a good speechifier!

Despite the welcome, we found a strong feeling against England, fostered by the Irish-Americans. Fantastic stories about the persecution of Irish people in England were in circulation, for American interest had been taken to fever-pitch by the famous Sweeney hunger-strike.

Irish Liberty Bonds were in demand, well-sustained by financial interests, and the most popular colour was green. Some English boxers pretended to be Irish and wore green knickers. When Jack Bloomfield had a Union Jack wrapped round his waist he nearly started a riot, and we had difficulty in persuad-

ing many people that the Irish were not being beaten
up and thrown into English jails ; that the English
as a whole were not bitter against the Irish, and lived
on excellent terms with them.

December 6th, the day of that momentous fight,
arrived inauspiciously. Snow prevented me (not for
the last time) from having a round of golf in the
morning. I always liked to wind up training with
golf, but that day I had to do a little in the gymnasium.

I also drank some egg-and-milk, with Al Thompson,
my chief sparring spartner. He is now settled in
Philadelphia, I believe.

'Lisbeth swears to this day that the drink was
drugged. Whether or no, we reeled home giddy and
sick. Al, in fact, did not properly recover for a long
while, and was knocked about mercilessly in one of
the preliminary bouts. I had too much to do to let
it worry me, as a matter of fact, for after weighing in
at seven o'clock I had to train like blazes to try and
get some of my superfluous weight off. Remember,
I had been forced to get to within ten pounds of
Sharkey's weight.

Imagine me, after stuffing puddings and anything
heavy to make the weight at seven o'clock, stripped
and fighting hard to get rid of it before nine ! I don't
know how much I managed to lose, but I do know
I felt more sluggish than I wanted when at last I
stepped into the ring for my first fight in America.

CHAPTER XII

SHADOWS

PERHAPS IT WILL BE AS WELL IF I GO BACK A LITTLE
to the preliminaries of the Sharkey bout before
describing the contest; one that must surely have
made a record in the number of different opinions it
roused.

I had been several months without a fight and, in
truth, without any serious training, for the weight
conditions of the bout, virtually demanded by the
boxing laws of Wisconsin, made it difficult to train
at all. The different rules for boxing in the various
States is one of the things that always makes it hard
for an English boxer to find his feet in America, and
it contributes in no small measure to the lack of
understanding between boxing devotees on the two
sides of the Atlantic. But there was one factor common to each State at that time : that was the method
of counting points, and the habit of making a bout a
" no-decision " one, leaving it to the Press to give its
opinions as to the result of the fight.

Unfortunately I knew very little of this.

Looking back, it is obvious that I should have
understood it more clearly, from my experiences with
Pal Moore and the other Americans I had met in
England. Against that, however, were the several

hundred English fights I had had : my ingrained understanding of the points of boxing, had been learned from the booth to the Albert Hall, without finding any serious variations.

The last thing I want to do, when writing about the much-discussed early days of the American tour, is to create the impression that I do not consider their methods fair, or their behaviour unsporting. It is perhaps difficult not to create that impression when dealing with facts as they appeared to me, and so it will be as well if I give, now, my sincere opinions of the fight-game in America, particularly on the reactions of the Press and the public to it.

There is, I think it will be generally admitted, a small section of that Press and public hostile to English boxers, either from prejudice or super-patriotism—aided at that time by the Irish trouble. But the vast majority are as scrupulously fair as in England. Perhaps, I should say, as I have always found them in England ; American fighters in our country doubtless feel much the same as I did over there. Backed by the sedulously cultivated publicity (let's say ballyhoo again !), however, the hostile section seems, to the stranger, to be much more powerful than it is.

Again, those laws differing from State to State are difficult for the newcomer to understand, but are naturally easy for the native who has been brought up to them. A particular example of these problems is the trouble I had to get the Sharkey bout signed and settled.

I heard and read a volume of criticism, that had I been easily affected, would have worried me a great deal. The habit of disparaging English fighters in the Press was well-developed. But not once did I meet face to face anyone who was other than pleasant, genuinely friendly and helpful. It was like living in two worlds. The hospitality was at times even embarrassing.

Certainly I might have been in another world, for it was bitterly cold—colder than I had ever known it. All these factors contributed to the way the Sharkey fight went.

These, then, were the ruling conditions prior to the fight at Milwaukee, and it would be difficult to conceive anything more calculated to disturb that detachment so vital to a boxer in the ring.

Sharkey contributed more, for he is one of the most unorthodox fighters I have ever met. He was a " half minute " fighter, covering up each round until the last half-minute, and then going at you with everything he had. He was a good-looking man for a boxer, but as tough and powerful as you could want.

I do not think there would have been any doubt of the verdict in England, but as it was officially " no-decision," the Press let fly next morning. I had proved a great disappointment; Sharkey had been an easy winner all the way; this and a dozen other sweeping statements, all condemnatory. One small voice in the wilderness did call:

" He demonstrated beyond doubt that he is the greatest fighter of his weight who had ever donned the mittens within memory of the oldest present-day fight-fans."

But that was practically the only pleasant thing the Press had to say. There were, mind you, plenty of people who gave me all the encouragement I needed : once again I can stress the vital difference between the ballyhoo, and the personal element. But there, after nearly five months without fighting, after looking forward to the trip as I had never anticipated anything in my life, was what appeared to be a complete eclipse.

The worst of it was I was convinced I had beaten Sharkey comfortably.

However, we had to accept things as they were, and not as we wanted them. I think we would have been in a lot worse position than we were but for the many English and Welsh friends we met from time to time.

Talbot O'Farrell, then at the height of his fame, frequently met us, and we often had his fine tenor as a free entertainment. Moreover, Otto Borchert did his best to infuse some cheerfulness into us—and I think he succeeded. The monotony of training, without the certain knowledge that there would be a fight fairly soon, had a depressing effect.

Training at the same gymnasium were two American boys, Pinkie and Richie Mitchell. They constantly jollied us.

" What is it, Jimmy, a funeral you're going to ? "

" It'll be your funeral if you're not careful."

"Listen to him! He'll even fight hicks like us, now."

The " hicks " managed to relieve a lot of the gloom and I hope they realised how grateful we were. Mr. Andrews, of Milwaukee, was never at a loss for a laugh and a good story. On the whole things weren't so bad, but unpleasant facts had to be faced.

The Sharkey affair had made promoters cool off abruptly : it looked as though it was going to be difficult to get another fight until the first at the Sportsmen's Club. I think it would have been but for the surprising changes, after a few weeks, that came over the Press. Why and how it was I don't know. Perhaps Referee Walter Houlihan had been talking, for he told me a week later that he thought I had won.

Houlihan was a capable and fair referee, and any opinion voiced by him carried considerable weight. The referee problem in boxing, on both sides of the Atlantic is a big one, of course, for as in many sports it is not always easy to get a man who is not only efficient, but also strictly impartial.

The trouble is that many are not consciously aware of any preference for one man against another. There are practically no referees in important boxing who are deliberately unfair, for a very good reason. No controlling body will use a referee known to give improper verdicts.

Well, the Press was veering round, with no apparent reason, even before I had fought again. I think it is the result of a tremendous " keying up " about the time of a crisis, a tension that gradually relaxes, allowing the judges to see the real facts clearer after the event. Here are two comments that made me feel that I was not being pointed out with a finger of scorn. The first from the *Milwaukee Sunday Sentinel* (after one or two bouts) was particularly pleasing because this paper had been fervent in its support of Sharkey, and never mentioned his name without adding : " the conqueror of Jimmy

Wilde." (That was a back-handed compliment, if you like !)

Said the *Sentinel* some weeks later :

" Jack Sharkey, the Eastern lad who got away with a lucky decision against Jimmy Wilde on the occasion of the foreigner's first appearance in the United States, has been matched to meet the English champion in London, for which he will receive fifteen thousand dollars in cash, three round trip tickets, *and the nicest, cleanest and most effective trouncing he ever got in his young life !*

" Sharkey cannot beat Wilde over the twenty round route, and in a foreign country. He was mighty lucky to have gotten the decision over Wilde when he did. Surely Wilde's later performances all showed him to be much better normally than he was the night he met Sharkey here, and on that occasion his wife, his manager, and some of his other friends, declared they had never seen him fight such a poor battle.

" Sharkey is a good lad but many think (*and the writer is one of them*) that Wilde is better."

My italics !

That, at that stage, showed me the most important thing about American sporting journalism. Their own men are held up to shoot at just as much as the English, or any other foreign fighter.

Before the *Sentinel* report, however (I did not at the time have an opportunity of telling the writer how much I appreciated it, and I hope he reads this), came a blunt announcement, two weeks after the Sharkey battle, from Jack Veioch, the International

News Service Sporting Editor. Veioch had always been renowned for his caustic writing:

"Had Wilde and Sharkey met in England it is altogether probable that owing to the English system of scoring points, Jimmy would have received an edge from perhaps a majority of those who would have been at the ringside. *But Jimmy's in our backyard now, and, as the saying goes, when you're in Rome, etc.* . . ."

My italics again.

Everything else apart, it was evident I should have to readjust my methods, in part at least. It was equally clear that I dare not put on weight again, for it slowed me down far too much. Hughes and 'Lisbeth were in full agreement. I think Veioch's brief, blunt statement was a deciding factor.

I was still training at Milwaukee, and, while there, an amusing thing annoyed me for a short while. A newspaper man approached me, talking of my next fight.

"I haven't fixed anything yet," said I.

"That so? You're boxing Carl Tremaine at Cleveland on January 1st, Jimmy."

"I know nothing about it," I retorted, "you can deny the reports."

He did not, and I was glad: for Matt Hinkle, the one promoter who had remained keen, had wired confirming a fight with Tremaine, who had been suggested as my opponent several times. Matt Hinkle and his enthusiasm were a grand stand-by in those days. I went into training with my tail up, helped in no small measure by a letter from ex-bantam-weight

champion Johnny Coulan. Coulan had already met
me, insisted on our being photographed together, and
proved he was going to be a good friend. I had read
several newspaper reports in which he had disparaged
me, but I was already beginning to doubt the authen-
ticity of them : I had been bitten when talking a little
about Johnny Dundee at the ringside. My companion had proved to be a reporter, and I was recorded
to have :

" . . . thought little of Dundee. The tiny
Briton is a cocky little chap, and talks flatteringly
of his own ability."
Brrrrh !

Johnny Coulan wrote :

" . . . I am sure you have been in the fight
game long enough to take no notice of reports
of that kind. I sincerely believe, if you met
Sharkey again there would be a different story to
tell. . . .

" I respectfully suggest that as long as there
are smaller men in this country why not grab at
them ? Take Frankie Mason and Tremaine for
instance . . . and by the way do not forget yours
truly. . . ."

Coulan had several other pleasant things to say
and suggested if he and I could not stage a bout in
America, we did at one of the English clubs later.
Unfortunately this did not come off : and by
the way, contract difficulties prevented me having a
return fight with Sharkey, one of the great regrets
of my life.

Just as we felt we were getting on, another blow

came. The Cleveland authorities this time vetoed the Tremaine fight on technical grounds. So many bouts were allowed each season, and this one would exceed the limit.

It was not easy to be cheerful, although an instructive thing happened when I had a three-round contest at the gym with Young Marino. I pulled off a lot of fancy work in the " work-off," dodging him, forcing him to miss, in short showing all the tricks of exhibition fighting. The spectators (remember they had paid admission fees) went into ecstasy : they *wanted* exhibition fighting. It was a repetition of the " verdict " from the crowd when Young Dando had boxed an exhibition with me many years before in the old country.

Christmas Day was miserable, cold and lonely. We did not once venture out, and we were beginning to think the whole tour would flop. But Boxing Day lived up to its name, for we had a visit from that grand old-timer, Tommy Sullivan, the only man who had ever knocked out Abe Attell. Sullivan was matchmaker for the St. Louis Athletic Club, and five minutes after his arrival he had matched me with Johnny (Babe) Asher, who had done remarkably well with the Allied Expeditionary Forces, both in the trenches and the boxing contests.

Sullivan lost no time in getting down to business.

" I'm told you're thinking of going to California, Jimmy."

" Yes, there's nothing to do here."

" Will you fight ? "

" Yes, that I will ! " The words gave me a real kick.

" Well, then, what about Johnny Asher, at St. Louis ? Eight rounds and I'll talk terms later."

" I'll fight Asher," I said, and 'Lisbeth suggested Sullivan might like some English tea.

Somehow depression insisted, however ; our landlord, an excellent fellow who had done everything possible to make us feel happy and at home, died unexpectedly. I was upset, and not only because it naturally delayed training. His widow and children were grief-stricken, and our little party was affected by their sudden loss.

Serious training did a great deal to relieve my mind. Determined to get as fit as a man could do, I arranged for Al Thompson and Ted Jamieson, the former thirty, the latter sixty pounds above my weight, to spar with me. I think at the time of the Asher contract I would gladly have agreed to fight Dempsey, then at the height of his fame.

Among other sparring partners was Young Dennis, an American who, during the preliminaries of the Frankie Mason-Sammy Marino fight that I went to see, met Billy Whelan, of St. Paul. It was a grand fight, and I gave Dennis eight of the ten rounds ; so did several of the papers, but one declared next day that Whelan had won. There was absolutely no logic in such a decision, and it softened my own experiences a great deal. Every day I was getting to know America better and growing to like it.

It was a day's train journey from Milwaukee to St. Louis, but I had been assured there was no likelihood of snow, and consequently every likelihood of golf. Golf was getting something of a craze with me, and I was more disappointed than I can say when St.

Louis celebrated my arrival with the first snow of the season. However, it was not too thick for walking; so I walked.

I walked into more trouble, too. For once, there was no suitable training quarters available, for the local Racquets Club offer was useless as they had not the equipment necessary. The only available place was the Business Men's Gymnasium, where Johnny Asher was training. I still could not get used to the idea of training with an opponent, and although I did exercises there, I cut out all boxing work. Meanwhile the weather was vile, and just before the fight a veritable blizzard descended. I was offered a lift to the fight by a friendly gentleman whose name I forgot, and the driver took a wrong turning.

After frantic efforts the others had to let me get out and walk until we could find some other way of reaching the Coliseum. For half an hour they had struggled to free the car from snow, while I had been muffled up inside.

At another time the experience would have worried none of us, for I had been used to roughing it often enough, but to put up a convincing show against Asher was vital and I was getting worried myself. Better to walk and get cold, said I, than be late for the fight.

We arrived in good time after all and I felt none the worse for the misadventure. I knew that Asher was a good lad although he had only been fighting a few years. As a matter of fact, the Zulu Kid was the only man who had ever knocked him off his feet.

The contest, as usual, was a no-decision one, of eight rounds: and we had to rely on the Press again. My one aim was to make sure there could be no possible arguments. This time (St. Louis having no boxing laws) I had been able to train down to my best weight, giving Asher, at 115½ pounds, over sixteen pounds.

I was told that the crowd was the biggest seen at the Coliseum, but I had nothing on my mind but Babe Asher. He came at me like a whirlwind, the accepted American form of attack, but he had shown what he could do in the first round. I remember a tremendous feeling of relief : I *could* do what I liked with a popular American fighter !

As a matter of fact, I could not. I knocked Asher off his feet several times, his face was plastered in his own blood, and in the fourth round I missed an opportunity when Asher went down for a long count, and I leaned against the ropes to let him get on his feet properly before wading in again. This move brought salvoes of cheers from the crowd : one might liken the attitude to that of the billiards player who refuses to pot the white. Strictly speaking, to pot the white is in the game, and a man is a fool not to do it. But in amateur billiards it's not done, any more than I had been taught that it was " done " to wait over a man in order to finish him the moment he had both knees off the canvas.

Asher kept on his feet most of the time. He had a particularly long and narrow chin, and I could not find the right place to hit it for a knock-out. That worried me, for it suggested my timing was at fault, but it was obvious there was no need to be greatly worried. There was not even a murmur of dissent from the opinion that I had won easily and, although the long-distance newspapers were cooler than the locals, there was a growing conviction that I possessed more ability than I had so far shown.

Asher, by the way, always gave himself away by telegraphing his punches, and I knew whenever he was coming. Without that one fault he would have made a much more effective fighter than he was, and I could certainly never wish to meet a man with more spirit. I liked Asher, and I think the feeling was reciprocated. He admitted lugubriously that he had never been hit so hard in his life, and he did not know how he had managed to go the whole course.

I have seldom been interested so much in a boxer, but I think the biggest bond between us was some advice I was able to give on reducing the swelling of an ear I had knocked about—as much as Tancy Lee had knocked mine, years back. The specific worked and a cure for swollen ears is in great demand among fighters, who are surprisingly extremely self-conscious about facial scars.

Well, I had started a " come-back." It is interesting, I think, now, to realise that in a few short months in America I had come to accept the fact that I was not reckoned a champion, as I had been in England, and that I had to " get back " in order to establish myself properly in that country. But now that I was getting to understand the people I felt more confident. I should get a square deal, whatever else, and that is always a tremendous fillip.

CHAPTER XIII

★

GETTING BACK

SOON AFTER THE ASHER FIGHT THERE WAS A CONTEST with Mike Ertle at Milwaukee on February 19th. Ertle's reputation was a good one, and I was glad I managed to put him down in three rounds, my first " decisive " victory in the States. It was not long afterwards before David Hughes managed to get a match with Micky Russell, in Jersey City.

It had been cold enough before the Sharkey fight : the Russell weather was worse, with the streets glazed with ice, cars and pedestrians skidding helplessly. Naturally the size of the crowd was disappointing, the mystery being the number who did venture out. The big hall was gaily decorated with flags of all nations, but the only Union Jack was about my waist. We had to get it in somewhere ; and it was the Press that commented caustically on the decorators' lack of impartiality, without pointing out the growing strength of the pro-Irish faction.

Russell had a tremendous reception : surely Dempsey even at that time could not have had a better one. I remember smiling as I went to the ring, preceded by a colossus of a policeman nearly twice my height. My seconds in that fight looked after Russell's bandages, and Monteith, Russell's chief, returned the courtesy. This was something of an innovation at the time.

In some ways Russell was disappointing : I had a feeling that he was stage-struck and I believe he could have found more to show against another fighter than he did with me. He hardly seemed to try to defend himself, but like all the Americans, he had remarkable toughness. I have rarely hit a man so heavily and so mercilessly, yet getting so little back ; but Russell was on his feet until the end of the eighth round, when the referee stopped the fight. In the seventh he had seemed dazed coming from his corner, and I remember one terrific right punch to the chin that lifted him off his feet and draped him over the rope, like a shirt over the clothes line. It was just after that that the referee said : " That's enough," and at the same time Monteith's towel came flying over.

There was some light relief during the early rounds, for Russell's supporters gave him vociferous advice and, after a while, woke up to the fact that I was acting on it. Thus : " Your left, Micky ! " Over went my left. " Now your right ! " And I obliged. " Now up the kitchen ! " And obligingly I sent a right to the stomach. The advice stopped abruptly soon afterwards.

A fortnight after the Russell fight, on March 3rd, I met Patsy Wallace, and gained further insight into the tricks of boxing. The contest was a six-round no-decision one at Philadelphia, which is some two hours' train journey from New York. Philadelphia always struck me as being one of the most spacious cities in the States. The City Hall in particular is a wonderful building, while there was an air of prosperity about everything and everyone that was pleasant if not ostentatious.

Twenty-five policemen of the Quaker City were needed to keep the crowd in order! The National Athletic Club was literally besieged, and I was assured that a great section of the crowd was not interested in boxing, but craved to see the " Mighty Atom "—or, as an American critic once said, the fastest slow man in boxing : this latter chiefly because the American fashion of boxing was much faster to look at than mine, particularly the Italian variation, and by contrast I must have looked a caterpillar.

It was grand to hear the roars that greeted my arrival in the ring. The clouds had rolled away. I might have been back at the N.S.C. in England, or the Albert Hall. I think 50 per cent of the crowd— of which 99 per cent was American—was with me, and that is a mighty fine encouragement in an " away " match. But Patsy, naturally, had an equally vociferous welcome : the crowd seemed set for hilarity, and probably it would not have taken a great deal to set them for anger. I remember one tremendous bellow as Patsy stepped into the ring :

" Go in and eat 'im up, Patsy ! Go in and eat 'im ! "

I had to smile.

There is a danger of giving this six round contest more space than it really deserves, but it was remarkable in many ways. I am sure Wallace did not seriously think he could knock me out, and after the usual whirlwind " Wop " start, he concentrated on avoiding me all he could, his one idea being to last the distance. He crouched all the time, moving fast, and was difficult to hit. But now and again I was able to break through his cover-up and paste him pretty soundly. Patsy did not seem to have any idea of stopping me, and in the first three rounds I think he was perilously close to going down for keeps.

Then he invented a variation in tactics.

It was more likely that he had worked it out beforehand. The first effort completely deceived me : it looked convincingly like an accident. After I had smashed two or three rights to his face he ducked and went through the ropes. I went to stop him from falling out of the ring, but saw that he was gripping the middle rope and was hanging half in and half out, solely to get a breather, and to stop me from hitting him. This novel manœuvre was repeated several times ! I did not hit him while he was hanging although, Patsy being technically in the ring, it would have been justified. The officials afterwards confirmed this. Such a blow, however, would have been misunderstood by the crowd and I did not want to cause trouble of any kind.

I had two pieces of bother I have never met before nor since. The dressing-room accommodation was not all it might have been, and water had streamed on the floor, soaking the soles of my shoes. I had had no opportunity of drying them, with the result that sawdust stuck on them like gritty snow. This, naturally, did not make it easy to move about the ring. One moment I felt I had two or three pounds hanging on me, the next it would shake off and go flying over the ring. To make it worse, in the fourth round my glove split.

I could do nothing. There was not a spare pair

available, and I had to carry on with my right thumb sticking through the glove. I did not hit as hard as I wanted, as I might have injured the hand. I had usually been fortunate in avoiding any severe finger injury, chiefly because I would never let a blow connect unless it went with the full, rounded knuckle. Through a glove, a knuckle blow can never do the slightest damage to the hand.

Here I was, then, with shoes like clod-hoppers and a split glove.

When I met Wallace again, later on, my glove split for the second time, one of the oddest coincidences I have experienced.

I was particularly anxious to put Wallace down for the count, and waded right into him in the sixth round. Half-way, damp sawdust sent me slithering and I went down instead.

Wallace had pushed a gentle right towards me at the moment and the roar from the crowd made it quite clear that they thought he had knocked me off my feet. He subscribed to the opinion afterwards, but I do not think that after round three he had a knock-out punch left, and he had clinched more than any fighter I had met. In fact the only way to make him fight was to stand still and let him come at me !

Knock-down or not, the Press and the public were pleased with the exhibition and I was particularly happy when a little crowd of Britons of incomparable memory—Wilkie Bard, Talbot O'Farrell, and two old friends from Aberdare then appearing in the States—decided to look me up. There was a general celebration, to the detriment of our supply of tea. I keep mentioning the tea, but believe me a cup of it brought back vivid memories of home.

The promoters offered me a return bout when I saw them next day and I accepted gladly. Before then, however, I had the Toledo fight with Frankie Mason on March 11th, only eight days ahead.

We approached Toledo in fear and trembling ; or precious close to it. We had been warned in every place we had fought that it was the grimmest spot in the States, and fantastic stories reached us about the certainty that something would be arranged to stop me from winning. Well, we took the proverbial pinch of salt with these tales, but there are limits to the amount of salt available and I think our party was prepared for anything, from kidnapping to attempted murder.

★

REPUTATION RESTORED

TO ADD TO OUR DIFFICULTIES, THE FIGHT WITH FRANKIE
Mason, of Fort Wayne, was undoubtedly the most
important of the American contests, for Frankie was
the only man who could contend for the title. He was
my own weight, with a reputation not unlike my own.
Giving away anything from ten to twenty pounds, as
I had been doing, had made sure that the title—the
only one England held at the time—was safe even if
I lost. This time it could be taken from me.

Here is the table of our respective sizes :

	MASON	WILDE
Age . . .	30 years	28 years
Weight . .	107 lbs.	106 lbs.
Height . .	5 ft. $2\frac{1}{2}$ ins.	5 ft. $2\frac{1}{2}$ ins.
Reach . .	$65\frac{1}{4}$ ins.	68 ins.
Chest (normal) .	$30\frac{3}{4}$ ins.	$32\frac{1}{2}$ ins.
Chest (expanded) .	36 ins.	$34\frac{1}{2}$ ins.
Neck . . .	$13\frac{3}{4}$ ins.	$12\frac{3}{4}$ ins.
Thigh . .	$16\frac{1}{2}$ ins.	$15\frac{1}{2}$ ins.
Waist . . .	26 ins.	22 ins.
Calf . . .	$11\frac{1}{2}$ ins.	$10\frac{1}{4}$ ins.
Ankle . .	$8\frac{1}{4}$ ins.	$8\frac{1}{4}$ ins.
Biceps . .	11 ins.	$10\frac{3}{4}$ ins.
Forearm . .	$10\frac{1}{4}$ ins.	$10\frac{3}{4}$ ins.
Wrist . .	$6\frac{3}{4}$ ins.	$6\frac{1}{2}$ ins.

So there was not a great deal in it, as you can see.

I was looking forward keenly to the fight, and the others kept a great deal of their anxiety away from me, although some of it naturally leaked through. I was inclined to think there was some exaggeration, and that proved more than the truth. Practically none of the fears were justified, and I was 'accorded as warm a welcome in Toledo as anywhere in the States—and in England for that matter—while I could not ask for a fairer deal than I had from the authorities, despite one fierce argument that lasted for a week or more, and at one time threatened to cause the contest to be cancelled.

Probably the warnings we had had made David Hughes adamant on this point, which was an important one : the choice of the referee. The promoter was Mr. Ad Thatcher—a rough diamond with a sound heart if ever there was one, yet a man about whom a great deal of gossip has circulated, as gossip will in the fight game. He took David's list of four acceptable referees to the Toledo Boxing Commission. He had warned us that they would be annoyed, and they were ! So much so that he boarded our train as we went through Toledo from Milwaukee, telling us that, if we insisted, there would be no fight. The Commission wanted Mr. Ollie Pecord, a local referee who had looked after the Dempsey-Willard fight— after a spot of bother, for there had been another protest.

There was nothing at all against Pecord, as far as we knew : he was a local man, and we naturally preferred someone quite independent. There is no need to go into the whole business, but when we reached

Toledo and David met the Commission, he was a long
way from popular. I believe he claimed a " paternal
interest " in me, asseverated there was nothing personal
against Pecord, but quietly insisted (David was quiet
about everything) that I would only fight with one of
those four referees. I remember he turned to the
Mayor, after a long discussion, saying :

> " No doubt I am wrong, in being so obstinate,
> but this is an important fight and if I change my
> mind at the eleventh hour and anything happened
> to Jimmy's detriment I should never forgive
> myself."

I think the Commission argued for five hours
before finally submitting, and we were all jubilant
about the " victory." The chosen referee, Mr. Ed
Smith, of the *Chicago American*, had been no more than
lukewarm after the Sharkey contest, and was
certainly not an enthusiastic Wilde fan. In fact I
think he was convinced I would not win. I know Ad
Thatcher was, although both were naturally pro-
American, and wanted to see the title in the States.
Nevertheless we had absolute confidence in Ed
Smith's fairness, although but for the grim warnings
we might not have insisted on him.

The odds were slightly in my favour, but one of
the most pleasant things imaginable helped me just
before the fight. Some six hundred Milwaukee
enthusiasts came three hundred miles to support me.
I wished every one could have the freedom of Tylorstown conferred on him !

There was one incident that worried us. Mason's
friends were very confident that he would win,

and friendly towards us. A few hours before the fight one of them brought along a cake, which looked very good indeed.

Now that provoked a delicate situation.

To refuse was to insult the hospitality of the others ; to accept was to endanger my fitness in the ring. Our refusal did rather upset the Mason camp, I'm afraid, but we stuck to it.

Some strong Mason partisans decided to take it out of 'Lisbeth at the ringside. They sat just behind her, pulling her hair, tipping her hat forward and making remarks about the " Wizard " which annoyed her. The upshot of this comes later.

Milwaukee proved that it had adopted me in earnest by sending as a second a tremendous policeman, Captain Higgins, who had previously seconded Freddie Welsh. Higgins was a jovial man, but quite prepared to stop any trouble that might develop. The fact that Milwaukee believed trouble possible shows we were not suffering from any of those complexes ! Higgins chuckled afterwards and declared :

" And I wasn't wanted at all ; it was a waste of a journey ! "

Frankie Mason was obviously going to try and tire me by fighting a retreating battle in the early stages, with a little clinching to help out. (Clinching is gradually creeping from the big men to the little 'uns, I'm afraid : I would like to see it abolished in every boxing country.) However, I had fought a hundred contests with an opponent of exactly the same state of mind, and it had never worked before. Frankie soon realised it would not, for I managed to get close and rattle him several times in those early rounds. He came back well, putting all he knew into a fierce stand-up fight that had the crowd delirious; and in the fifth round he put everything into his effort.

I think the round was even: but in the sixth I could see he had shot his bolt. In that fight, particularly, that was a grand feeling, yet although I tried all I knew to stop him from lasting the limit, he lasted.

I think it was in round six that, in a quiet spell from the crowd, I heard a familiar but angry voice shout from the ringside, in Welsh:

" If you don't finish him, Jimmy, I'll come and do it myself. They're giving me a hell of a time here ! "

There could have been no keener incentive and I was told afterwards that Frankie did not take another round. He knew nothing of the rumpus at the ringside, not knowing Welsh.

In round eleven I thought I had him at last. A left hook to the stomach had sent him staggering and dazed, side-stepping and dodging cleverly but automatically. I found room for a right to the chin, but mistimed it a fraction: Frankie immediately dropped into a clinch. I was almost desperate, for I wanted to floor him, but before I could get home with a finisher the gong went.

In round twelve Frankie was severely cautioned for clinching, but muttered an answer that he was determined to last the fight now he had gone so far !

He lasted it : but there was not a single argument against the popular verdict for me (thank heavens !), while Ollie Pecord showed he bore no grievance by admitting I had won easily. Ed Smith, the referee, wrote next day :

" The reason why Mason was there in the ring when the match was ended was because he could run faster ! "

That put the finishing touch to my contentment, for Smith had been equally caustic about me after the Sharkey bout. Mason himself admitted that he had under-estimated me, and he cheerfully wished me well.

So that fight finished as I had hoped, but for the failure to knock my man out—a difficult thing in a comparatively short bout—and I had five weeks' rest to come. I felt I needed it before going to Canada to meet my old opponent, the Zulu Kid. This was a ten rounds " no-decision," but the papers were making up for lost time with a vengeance and I was allowed to see all the reports !

My first bout with Zulu Kid had been a sensation in England, and had enabled me to win the world title. I hoped there was no doubt now in the States that the title was worthily mine, but I knew that the slightest faltering against the Kid would swing the popular ideas round, and I had no desire to take the slightest chance. I was confident enough, for I knew his methods, and I did not seriously think he would be able to offer serious opposition.

Nevertheless I trained assiduously, regretting that the snow prevented me from playing my beloved golf. It might be fitting, while approaching the second fight with Zulu Kid, to talk a little more fully on the advantages of meeting a man who had already faced me in the ring.

Each boxer has his tricks, little mannerisms some of them ; others deliberate and well-conceived tactics. There is a thrill in watching the meeting between two hitherto unmatched boxers. You can never be sure which of them has a little something up his sleeve, and you cannot guess how one man is going to face up to the unknown elements in the other's repertoire. In a long first fight—eight rounds or more, anyhow— you can be sure that your opponent is showing everything, but in a second meeting the only likelihood of a surprise method of attack or defence is that your opponent has conceived a new idea, and practised it assiduously.

It was possible that the Zulu Kid had something new, but I was not convinced that this would be the, case, particularly because of his specialised method— ducking almost down to his knees in defence and, in my opinion, robbing himself of just that little extra needed for attack.

We went to Ontario on a little ferry that moved sluggishly across the wide St. Lawrence River, arriving two days before the fight. As usual, it was not easy to get training in, for the citizens were anxious to show us the sights. Windsor is a pleasant city, but anything less like the original in England it would be hard to imagine.

We had a good crowd, and Zulu Kid was obviously as glad to see me as I was to see him.

" How're you, Jimmy ? Better than ever, I hear."

" As good, I hope," I said. " You're looking fit."

" I'll show you something ! "

But if he had had anything to show me he certainly would not have said so, and the old ducking tactics were quickly in evidence. It was a good fight from my point of view and from that of the crowd, but I was glad there was no argument about the popular verdict afterwards. It went the whole ten rounds of the " no-decision " kind.

Coming back on the ferry, we seemed to take longer than on the first trip. It was queer to be out there in the middle of the river with a peculiar feeling that the ferry might not be as water-worthy as it should be. But we reached the other side without any suggestion of trouble and lost no time in getting back to the Wauwatosa flat.

Not long after this, Battling Murray sent through a challenge.

Murray was a man with a deservedly big reputation, and I was glad to accept the fight. Although he was an Italian from Philadelphia, the fight was staged at Camden, N.J., and we had a crowd of nine thousand people. That club, by the way, is deserving of special mention if only because the " no-smoking " rule was strictly maintained. It was the first time in my life, except in the open air, that I had fought in a clear atmosphere, and I sometimes wonder whether it would make much difference if the rule were always enforced. It was pleasanter to enter the hall, but once in the ring I don't think any fighter takes much notice of atmospheric conditions other than those his opponent makes for him. On the other hand, I was so used to smoke that my indifference was probably habit. If one could always be sure of clearness it might do the fighters more justice.

Sensation came quickly, but I cannot, in all honesty, blame the no-smoking rule. A vicious left to the chin shook me, and I was telling myself that this boy Murray was dangerous when I found myself on the floor, feeling dazed. It was a nasty jolt, so early in the fight, but I got up quickly, clinched for a moment to recover, and then stalled around. The blow had me groggy. My seconds told me so and I was more than ready to believe it.

What would have happened had Battling Murray not made a vital mistake I don't know. He decided to box at long range, which suited me down to the ground just then. Another whirlwind attack at the beginning of the second meeting might have made all the difference, but Murray did not know—or at least did not follow—the essentials of boxing tactics. Tactics often won me a fight that had looked like going the other way. For some time we boxed at a distance, a blow here and there keeping things warm. Round three brought him out with a rush again, probably on advice from his seconds, but I was fully rested and ready for anything he could show. I remember exulting when he came in obviously determined to mix it. I took him all over the ring, and he tried boring in at every opportunity, one blow sending me reeling backwards and bringing the crowd to its feet in excitement.

The cheering for Murray got under my skin a little. I remember rushing in and catching him with a right that started one of the fiercest rounds I have fought and, I was afterwards told, one of the fiercest seen at the Club. The crowd believed Murray held a winning chance, but he fell for a barrage of lefts that had him groggy and veered the fight round in my favour.

From that moment onwards Murray might have

been called a human skittle. He had shot his bolt after losing that chance and now his face was swelling and his ribs were scarred. The referee, Billy Rocap, and John Smith, the Club's chairman, stopped the fight simultaneously after Murray had hit the canvas three times in quick succession.

A technical knock-out again, and I felt that I was getting back nicely. Of the nine fights I had staged in (or near) the States until then, eight had been mine, and the only adverse " verdict " had been the Sharkey one. I think every paper in the country was prepared to say, after the Murray fight, that Sharkey could not have lasted another fight with me.

That feeling was like nectar.

But to remain on top of the world I had to keep winning. A dozen victories were nothing like so important as a single loss, even one which was open to discussion. That " must win " feeling is a strange one. It is probably keener in boxing than in any other sport, where the spotlight of publicity is centred on the ring for so brief a period, nothing before nor after that bout being of serious consequence. And remember, one single moment's relaxation can prove vital. Murray, for instance, might have managed to knock me out in that first round, and it would have been sensational enough to ruin all the good my previous victories had done. Mind, nerve, heart and body all working together like a finely-adjusted machine, and if one small component fails for a fraction of a second—finish, or at least a long climb back.

Murray challenged me again soon afterwards and, especially because of the first round, I was happy to sign a contract with him. But before that we had an

interlude on Freddie Welsh's Health Farm at Orangeburgh, a beautiful place just outside New York.

Talbot O'Farrell put in an appearance, with Fred
Dyer, the Welsh singer then touring the States, Gus
Wilson, who trained both Dempsey and Carpentier,
many others, both old and new friends. Freddie Welsh
died soon afterwards, and that Orangeburgh visit
was the last time I saw the idol of my boyhood dreams.

It was with something of a shock that we returned
to the Jersey City flat to find that champions and
others were all one with gentlemen of the burglary
profession, and that it had been stripped. We were
more angry than amused at first, for the police seemed
far more interested in me and boxing than in the
burglary, and it was with some effort we persuaded
them that our losses had been important enough to
investigate. Afterwards, although our silver, including several prizes, had gone forever, we saw the funny
side of it. The police were genial souls, if their
methods were strange to us.

Such things are bound to happen, and the Sportsman's Club did its best to make sure we were not
unduly perturbed. No one could have treated us
with greater friendliness, and I remember one particular night when a banquet was staged, with our little
party as the principal guests. 'Lisbeth was presented
with a silver dish, and I received a pair of silver loving
cups that remain among my most cherished
possessions.

Unfortunately I don't remember the personnel of
the gathering, but they cheered us up a great deal.
It was as well that we were having a brief lull from
fighting, however, for the generosity and hospitality

of the various enthusiasts made sleep more a matter of longing than anything else. Particularly do I remember visiting Sir David Llewellyn's suite at the Biltmore Hotel, New York. There we met Sybil Vane, the Cardiff singer, while soon afterwards, a guest with other new-found friends, Talbot O'Farrell popped up again.

On May 1st I had a new opponent in Bobby Dyson, at Lawrence, Massachusetts. Frankly I remember little about the contest, although it brought almost frantic enthusiasm from the crowd and the Press, except that I was forced by the rules to live three days in Lawrence before the fight, and taken to every conceivable function. The fight was for $8,000 and just before it someone said :

" Dyson's very hot, Jimmy."

" Well, I'm very fit," said I.

" Do you think you'll beat him ? "

" Well, I see no reason why I shouldn't," I said. " I'm fit enough to beat him."

" Ah, but he's a hot 'un, is Dyson," repeated my companion dubiously.

At the open-air weigh-in I saw the cameras from the film companies, a novelty in its way, and yet something not in the contract. So I had a word with an official, in the hope of increasing that $8,000.

" They can't use that, man. It isn't in the contract."

That caused a hullabaloo, and there was a lot of arguing and bickering, coupled with a suggestion that my contract had nothing to do with filming the show. I pretended anger.

" Isn't it then ? I won't fight if pictures are taken, I tell you. Unless . . ."

" Ah ! "

" For a consideration," said I. " Make it a thousand dollars, and I'll say no more."

Finally they made it $500 and with a great bustle the cameras were set. But Dyson went down and out early in round one, and the film rights were worth next to nothing !

The second fight with Murray in Philadelphia, on May 13th, was drawing near, and I had to get down to serious training. I remembered that previous bout only too well, particularly the long right-handed punch that had virtually finished him.

I remember asking 'Lisbeth if she remembered it : needlessly, for I think she remembered (and still does) far more about the fights than I do myself.

" And why ? " she asked.

" Because it's going to operate a lot earlier to-night," said I, a piece of bragging that did not get me a punch on the head as it deserved. Had it come, I would have had the laugh on 'Lisbeth.

Nevertheless, Murray had something that few of the others possessed. That typical whirlwind fighting of the Americans made him come in like a veritable tornado, and he shook me quickly with three hooks to the head. The crowd was on its feet again. Would Murray take his opportunity this time ?

Happily there was no more than a shaking in the punches, and I was not dazed. I can almost hear the roaring now.

" There he goes ! Put him away, Bat, put him away ! "

And Bat was after that all right, but he left his face open, and just before the gong I found a right that crashed into his jaw, lifting him off the canvas so that he glided several feet through the air. I think that was the heaviest punch I had landed on an American opponent, and how he came up for the second round I don't know.

But he did, and with a rush again. But he was comparatively easy to dodge, and I felt it was safe to fight it out with him on the bear-cat principle. Murray liked that until I drew back and let fly with a left hook. He hit the floor face downwards and stayed for several seconds, swaying to his feet on the count of eight. A light tap with a left sent him toppling downwards. I think the crowd would have liked another hook, but where was the need?

Referee Pat O'Brien waved me back to my corner, and then there started a positive free-for-all that showed me how I could rely on the enthusiasm of the American crowd. In fact they were so anxious to pat my back that it needed half a dozen policemen (sorry, cops!) using their batons to clear space for me to get back to the dressing-rooms.

Murray managed to find a smile despite his battered face, and came into me soon after. I wish all boxers would make a habit of that gesture, although it is not always possible.

At all events, Murray said pleasant things, and :

" When he socked me on the chin I thought my head was going to leave my shoulders ! "

Yet after a blow like that he had managed to get to his feet and come up for another round. There is more in fighting than meets the eye, more in most boxers than a battered face and unshapely hands.

'Lisbeth had enjoyed the brief fight, and she was particularly pleased because that night she sat next to Major J. A. Drexel Biddle, who had been partly responsible for the American tour. Major Biddle had expressed the opinion that " Jimmy's execution is marvellous . . . there has never been a small boxer of his class, not even Young Griffo."

For some reason or other, that is the kind of remark that always made 'Lisbeth feel the world was a little place made especially for her : and there have been times when she has been able to make me think so, too !

As a matter of fact, although favourable comparison with past giants of the ring always brings a glow of pleasure, it is nearly always inaccurate : I remember A. G. Hales, that husky writer and boxing enthusiast, writing in 1916 that to compare me with Young Griffo was absurd ; I was nowhere near the American at his prime. And both the Major and the author could back their beliefs by fierce arguments, as useless as the inevitable argument on the respective merits of Grace and Bradman.

.   .   .   .   .

Some things are very difficult to believe, and the restoration of that battered reputation of mine after the Sharkey bout was one of them. I had not been in the States many weeks, but long enough to understand the difficulties attending a boxing tour, more than long enough to have my ego slapped soundly, and nearly long enough to start suffering from an inferiority complex, although I don't think that phrase had been invented ; or, at least, it was not generally used, in 1920.

'Lisbeth, David Hughes, Benny Williams and others have admitted since that they were worried by the first two or three fights, and were afraid I would not be able to show the Americans all that I could do in England. But they did nothing at all to create that impression at the time and, surrounded by them— how they watched over me!—I do not think I was fully aware of the storm of disparagement that had been roused. I would like to know how many of the more caustic newspaper reports were tactfully destroyed before I managed to see them.

Looking after a champion boxer must be as bad as looking after a *prima donna ;* perhaps even worse. I am not surprised that of late boxers have thrown fits of temperament that have, unhappily, been misconstrued by the Press and public, on both sides of the Atlantic, and for that matter on the Continent. It seems to be generally admitted that a film star, an opera singer, a pianist, in fact anyone with an artistic reputation, can go temperamental when they like, and be whitewashed, even exploited. But let a fighter do the same, and he brings on his head a storm of abuse.

Yet preparing for fight after fight, knowing that a single failure can virtually destroy years of effort, in many cases knowing that not only a boxing career but a fortune stands to be won or lost, I think the boxer has more excuse than the others. It is true that far more fuss has been made of little spots of boxing bother since the War, but this is typical of every phase of life. The boxer has been exploited, just like every other sportsman.

The present-day boxer cannot move without

finding trouble of some kind. Small, even petty pinpricks at times ; but sometimes enough to make a saint see red. These have been far more rife of late than when I started championship fighting.

Well, my trio of adherents had saved me from that complex. Looking back, I find it surprising that I never seriously doubted the success of the tour, despite the initial set-backs ; but it remains a fact. And, again looking back, I can see how the confidence of 'Lisbeth and the others strengthened after the Russell bout. But they had made a very fine and convincing pretence all along.

When the pendulum did swing towards me, it came with a bounce. There is nothing half-hearted about approval or condemnation on the " other side." One humorously-minded sports writer (Thomas E. Rice, of the *Brooklyn Eagle*) watched the fight between Johnny Kilrain and Benny Valgar, at New Jersey. It was not an exhilarating contest, particularly for well known feather-weights, although Valgar clearly won. Afterwards Rice wrote :

> " If none of the lady cops are looking and any citizen were to offer us a bet we would wager one small doughnut to three large ones that Jimmy Wilde, the fly-weight champion of the world, could beat Kilrain, and if the odds were lengthened a bit we would bet a smaller dough-nut that Jimmy would beat Valgar ! "

That was one of the many aspects of the change-over of public opinion, and one of several that afforded us a laugh. Another was a perfect demonstration of proving black was white. The writer (I have forgotten

who) set out to show my equality with Dempsey!
This way:

103 lb. Jimmy Wilde fought Joe Lynch
           Lynch fought Joey Fox
           Fox fought Benny Valgar
           Valgar fought Johnny Dundee
           Dundee fought Benny Leonard
           Leonard fought Jack Britton
           Britton fought Micky O'Dowd
           O'Dowd fought Clay Turner
           Turner fought Battling Levinsky
           Levinsky fought Jack Dempsey 200 lb.

Q.E.D.

★

CHAPTER XV

AMERICAN FINALE

FOR MY LAST FIGHT OF THAT FIRST VISIT TO AMERICA, I had to cross the St. Lawrence River again, this time to Toronto for another bout with Patsy Wallace. In the first fight with Wallace you may remember that I broke my glove and another pair was not available. Exactly the same thing happened at Toronto, but this time I was not worried by wet shoes and clumps of sawdust.

The City Hall at Toronto is surely one of the loveliest and finest buildings in Canada. It is world-famous, while the city itself has a great deal to recommend it.

Despite the abnormal height of the buildings, which rules in Canada as well as in the States, there is an indefinable " British " atmosphere about Toronto, unless I was deceived by a feeling that I was on British soil. The hospitality of the people rivalled anything I had met in U.S.A. and for the few days before the fight I was forced to go on many " triumphal " tours through the red and cream brick buildings which attracted me so much. Incidentally, among the many friends we made there we have corresponded regularly with a doctor and his wife, who spared no effort to make our comparatively brief visit happy and comfortable.

There was, however, the same remarkable lack of understanding of the needs of training. There seems to be a general idea among people who are not in the fight game that all you need to prepare for a fight is half an hour's Swedish drill, a quick change, some boxing gloves, and visit to the ring.

I have deliberately avoided the subject of training as much as possible, for just as it is monotonous to the boxer, so it must be to the reader. It is one long series of road work (running and walking); sparring with bigger men than yourself, providing you're not a heavy-weight; the usual physical training routine, and above all, care with food. Even at my slight weight I dared not eat food that was fattening : it had to be muscle-building or nothing.

The biggest difficulty the trainer has to face with his charge is that inevitable monotony. Whatever we do to-day, we have to do to-morrow, and so on *ad infinitum*. Believe me, it is nothing like the fun that it sometimes looks. Golf provided me with a variety and an interest that would otherwise have been sadly lacking. A contented mind while training means, very often, success in the ring.

There is another angle to training and I found it particularly after the War, when as a boxer I had become more of a public figure. Crowds would come to watch the sparring—a constant stream of visitors, particularly Americans. Many of them assured me that those nights were better than the actual fights.

Police and military made up a large proportion of the visitors to the Workmen's Club, Tylorstown, where I sparred. It was there, too, that I first met Ben Hardwick, now one of the best of referees. And the same Bob Jones is steward of the Club—he has been there for over thirty years. But the crowds at Tylorstown were negligible when compared with those at the American gymnasia.

There is another bright side to the camp-work. The Press can always be relied upon to be present, and it is surprising how many friends a well-known boxer makes with the reporters. That leads me astray again to a factor that is equally apposite in all the countries where I have boxed. The Press is remarkably fair.

Seeing that I have made several caustic comments on U.S.A. newspapers, that may seem an inconsistent thing to say, but I am sure that, with a few exceptions, the sporting newspaper-writer says what he thinks. I may be as friendly with him as I am with my sparring partners and trainer, but if he thinks I am falling back, if he sees any little fault (or what he conceives to be a fault) it is in his column the morning after he has watched the training, while he reports a big fight with astonishing frankness, and with no thought at all to the feelings of the contenders.

All that is as it should be.

There are, undoubtedly, occasional cases of favouritism in the Press, but they are rare. And the difficulty of the champion fighter (or cricketer or tennis-player) is that the slightest fall from grace is greeted with a fanfare of trumpets, while there is always the next champion waiting, so to speak, round the corner. That probably explains why the papers cannot afford to be in any way prejudiced. A man might be on top of the world to-day, and to-morrow at the bottom. That is, perhaps, an exaggeration, although it is not far from the truth. Think for a few moments of the number of boxers who had been nine days' wonders and have then dropped out of the limelight completely, or have at best suffered from disparagement and, very often, weighty sarcasm.

If there is one thing the Press does not like it is swollen-headedness in a boxer. I don't mean over-confidence : a boxer would be useless without faith in himself. He can say what he likes about his chances of winning his next fight, and be reported *verbatim*, no matter how much bravado there might appear to be in his words. But once let him say : " I'm So-and-so, and I'll have you know it," and he asks for trouble. More often than not he gets it, and it is a fact that very few bumptious boxers have reached the top of the fighting ladder.

So much for asides on training, and the Press : I had best get back to Toronto and Patsy Wallace.

Wallace, as I have said before, was a peculiar man to box, with his queer covering style, and his ability to use the ropes to his own advantage, and to get a precious breathing space. In the early rounds of the bout he caught me unexpectedly on the upper lip, cutting it badly and, I afterwards discovered, breaking an artery.

I had no idea there was so much blood in my body.

All I could do, while it was flowing so freely, was to box and keep out of Patsy's reach. The blood poured down my mouth, chin and chest, even soaking my knickers. At the end of the round my seconds did what they could, but in those days the art of healing a wound temporarily had not reached the heights it

has to-day, and they could do little but keep wiping
the blood away, and cleaning me up.

" Sure you're all right ? " Al Thompson said.
" Don't take chances, Jimmy."

I intended to say : " I'm all right, yes," but all
I managed was :

" Ump-ump-ump."

" Quite sure ? " Al demanded.

" Ump-ump-ump."

I must have sounded convincing, for he worried no
more about it, and the gong went for the third round.
Again I boxed carefully, and Wallace was faced with
an unexpected question. He had, I know, planned
to keep on the defensive all the time, yet here was a
wonderful opportunity for him to come out into
attack. I think he was a little doubtful whether I
felt as bad as I looked, and he certainly did not try
to take advantage of the opportunity as much as he
might have done. It is impossible to say whether he
would have been really dangerous had he done so,
but I did look a lot worse than I was.

The bleeding stopped after two rounds and I made
sure that he did not catch my lip again. There was
little or nothing remarkable in the remaining rounds.
The fight went the whole ten, with the usual " no-
decision " terms, but the general verdict was in my
favour.

My last fight of the tour was over. Eleven bouts
and, since the Sharkey affair, hardly a challenge to the
general verdict in my favour. That was a grand
piece of knowledge.

Remembering that cut artery also reminds me of the
fact that, throughout my boxing days, I did not take

the precaution of wearing gum-shields. I was often advised to, yet I felt it was not necessary, and the best shield was my own defence. That may have made me better on defence, but I doubt it. None the less, in the course of my eight hundred and sixty odd fights I must have been hit in the mouth an average of ten times a fight—many more in some of them. That, by a simple process of arithmetic, adds up to nearly nine thousand blows in the face while in the ring, and discounts the other nine thousand or so that I must have had during training. Yet I still possess all my own teeth, and they are in good enough order.

From Toronto we went back to New Jersey. Only a few days remained for the preparations for the return trip and saying good-bye to the many friends we had made. Frankie Burns and his wife were with us and Peter Donellan, a great friend of mine and 'Lisbeth's. It was a queer feeling. I would have gladly stayed for another eleven contests, but there was the same difficulty in the States as there would be in England—a shortage of candidates. It was useless to keep fighting the same man over and over again, and few promoters were prepared to risk bouts with unknowns. On the other hand, I longed to see England and Wales once more. I think the whole of our party was, in truth, ready to get back.

I was more afraid of the weather than anything else.

I could not even pretend that I had enjoyed the trip on the *Baltic*, and we all prayed for better luck in the crossing on the *Adriatic*, a bigger and better ship, we had been told.

The last few days were memorable. There was a

constant stream of visitors, pressmen, boxing friends and others, to make us feel that the tour had been successful, and to assure us that it would not soon be forgotten. I wondered whether the same thing would have happened had I travelled to America when I first wanted to, and I could not help thinking of the fate of the *Titanic*. It was incredible, on board the *Adriatic*, to think that a great liner of that kind could have been sunk so disastrously, and with such dreadful loss of life. The only surprising thing, in fact, was that so many were saved.

The weather repaid us for the earlier drubbing.

We left New York in brilliant sunshine, sailing past that magnificent skyline again, thinking more of the friends we were leaving than those we would meet again in England. There were the usual crowds at deck tennis, and after the first two days I was able to take proper nourishment and a real interest in the life of the ship.

Among the other travellers whom I especially remember was the Crown Prince of Sweden. He was travelling incognito, but his identity was widely known. I found him a charming fellow, with an excellent command of English. He was a gay spirit, and during that trip, at least, took his responsibilities very lightly. He laughingly refused to admit that I could outbox him—but we kept our rivalry to deck-tennis.

The Prince enlivened the trip a great deal, and it passed quickly. By the third day we were all looking forward keenly to seeing England. The Isle of Wight, our first sign, seemed to bring a nostalgia we had not felt in the States, and the friendly bustling quayside at Southampton shouted a welcome in itself.

Among the friends and pressmen to meet us at Southampton was John Mortimer, an old friend from the South. Mortimer had once managed Joe Beckett, and apart from Teddy Lewis, I can imagine no man I would have preferred to look after my interests. We frequently exchanged week-ends with John Mortimer and his wife, at their Southampton home.

Mortimer and I agreed on Joe Beckett's qualities. Joe was a fine boxer, but not quite enough of a fighter to get just that little extra needed for a world-championship. I know his rugged ring-work (as well as his rugged face and bulky body) often created the impression that he was more fighter than boxer, but I don't think it was true.

How can one explain Joe's failures against the foreigners?

I am not thinking only of that Carpentier bout, when he fell for a comparatively simple trick in the first seventy seconds. Against British fighters he was really first-class, as he proved over and over again, but something seemed to stop him whenever he met a man from another country. He is not the only boxer to have suffered from the same inexplicable complex, and I am not the only contemporary of Joe's who believed that he never showed quite his best in the ring. Yet it could hardly be stage-fright and it was certainly not lack of courage.

Joe's left hook was a thing to remember, and was often devastating.

I saw a great deal of him while training at Farnborough during the War, and we frequently appeared in the week-end tournaments. He is as good-tempered and generous a man as you could wish to meet.

Well, I was in England once more, feeling as fit as ever and ready for anything. I hoped for a short holiday, and then another series of fights, but for a while, at least, strict training was to be forgotten.

CHAPTER XVI

★

CLOUDS AGAIN

I HAVE NOT YET TRIED TO SUMMARISE THE AMERICAN tour, and I wonder whether it would be wise. It was a remarkable spell, full of light and shadow; one moment feeling on top of the world, the next in the deepest gloom. I wonder if the experience of every stranger who goes to America with something of a reputation is the same? In many ways, used to the somewhat humdrum steadiness of England, it is disconcerting. In others it is tremendously exhilarating. There is a fascination to be found in the States that I have never discovered anywhere else and, while I cannot say I would rather live there than in Wales—or England as the case may be—I can easily understand the lure that takes so many people over there.

The contrast, compared with England, is everywhere. For instance, at Milwaukee we found a considerable German population, and as it was soon after the Great War it was not easy to get used to that. But what was stranger was the fact that there was not the slightest suggestion of ill-will towards them. Among that crowd of six hundred who journeyed from Milwaukee to Toledo for the fight with Mason there must have been two hundred Germans; naturalised Americans, it is true, but

222

feeling—as anyone must have felt—a sorrow for the plight of their native country. By far the most important international factor was the Irish problem. I wonder how much influence its misrepresentation has to do with such anti-English feeling as there is in the States to-day?

In England at that time a German would have been extremely unpopular; even a German-sounding name was suspect. In America it was of no account what nationality a man had owned before taking on American nationality.

Then there is the spaciousness of the country. In England we are all next-door neighbours; those tremendous railway journeys, the incredible wonder of the scenery, everything, in fact, was a contrast to the quiet green country-side of England and Wales. In my youth I had been impressed by our South Wales mountains. Those who want to be really impressed should spend a few weeks in the States. Everything is, from the scenery point of view, at least twice as fine as its reputation.

The weather, too, is entirely different. I still shiver mentally when I think of those snowy, icy nights when we left our quarters for a bout. Icicles hanging from every roof and wall, roads thick with ice, cars twisting round in circles every few yards, people walking gingerly along, risking a fall and a broken bone at each step. Not a rarity, mind you— after all, we have an occasional " silver thaw " and we do get ice-bound roads in England and Wales. But in America it lasted for weeks at a time; you began to wonder whether it would ever be different.

But despite this, it was an unforgettable tour.

Apart from the boxing there were the trips about the various big towns. I have not been able to do them all justice, but there were few disappointments.

Chicago is another town that reminded me of London, one of several in America that brought up the same comparison. It was not simply because they were big cities : New York could never appear to me like our own capital, while I have not had the same feeling in the larger industrial towns of England, Wales and Scotland.

I particularly remember three visits to large car-manufacturing factories. At that time mass-production was only in its infancy, and I do not think there was anything vaguely reminiscent of the Ford works in England. It seemed incredible that so many cars were being prepared for the road ; what on earth must the works look like to-day ?

The Studebaker and Cadillac works were of a different nature, although they had certain things in common with Ford's. The conveyor system, particularly, intrigued me. But my biggest wonder, as I have said, was the quantity of new cars going out of the factories every day.

I believe it is computed that there are ten times as many cars being manufactured to-day as there were in 1920, yet it rarely strikes one to stop and compare London in 1938 with that of twenty years ago. Creatures of habit, aren't we ? And at the risk of repeating myself too often, I can only say that America will always seem to be the country of contrasts : nothing else seemed so important.

I was to go there again, of course. History has told of that second trip, of which I know very little excepting that the weather was as hot as it had been cold before. Before the trip, however, there were things to do in the home country.

One of the earliest was a theatre contract, for four nights, with Rube Welch, who was very keenly interested in boxing, and who aimed to make up for the one disappointment in the American trip—the failure to get a bout with Pete Herman. I do not know why Herman refused to fight me over there, for I knew he was an exceptionally fine boxer, and I proved that afterwards. But for some reason he had never agreed to terms, although I certainly do not subscribe to the oft-voiced opinion that he was afraid to meet me : why should he have been ?

But this theatre business.

It was actually a rag, guying the boxing game : the photograph will give you some idea of just how it was guyed. I believe there were big crowds, but I doubt whether I had any talent for the stage—even hidden talent, despite my revue " experience " in the War days. That one four-night contract was the only one I signed then, at all events.

Rube Welch was confident he could get Herman to fight, although once C. B. Cochran had arranged for the battle at the Olympia and it had fallen through, much to his and my disappointment. It began to look, now, as though nothing would ever come of it, despite Welch's optimism.

For I was determined to retire.

I was nearly thirty, at the time, and thirty is a good age for any boxer. The constant tension, in and out of the ring, the impossibility of taking any liberties, was more of a strain than is generally admitted. Moreover

I had my two second loves : golf and snooker. People have said that I should have taken up snooker instead of boxing as a career, but I have grave doubts.

Retirement after nearly nine hundred fights in twelve years !

If there was a regret in my mind when eventually we decided to settle down in Wales, it was that I had never met Herman, virtually the only fighter of consequence near my weight whom I had never faced. However, I cannot say I felt it too keenly. I had had those eight hundred and sixty appearances in the ring and, though I say it as shouldn't, it was a record that will always give me pride. Tancy Lee, Pal Moore and Sharkey could all boast victories, although in my own mind I can admit only the Tancy Lee verdict. Call it stubborn if you like.

Moreover, although I could have had any number of additional fights with smaller men, who had everything to gain and little to lose, few of the really big fighters were anxious to meet me, and I had reached the stage when there had to be a reasonably good contest as well as an exceptional money interest to make me change my mind about retirement. It was absurd to keep fighting youngsters without an honest chance, although had there been a dozen serious challengers, I would have met them gladly. I realised that there would have to be long intervals between the fights, and three or four months' inactivity reduces the efficiency of a boxer at least twenty per cent ; such, at least, is my belief.

'Lisbeth was as anxious as I to see the end of it, and if Lewis and Hughes were disappointed, they accepted the decision with good grace.

We selected a house at Radyr, near Cardiff, and we called it Lonsdale, after that grand patron of the fight game. I had won the Lonsdale Belt for " keeps " and, in common with every boxer, I had a deep admiration for Lord Lonsdale.

I was not to know that, nearly seventeen years afterwards, he was going to be good enough to write an introduction to my memoirs.

I had never felt fitter, and with golf, snooker, some livestock, 'Lisbeth and an appreciable fortune, I had every reason to be content.

Then, out of the blue, came a cable from Rube Welch, offering a fight with Herman at the Royal Albert Hall. The actor-promoter had signed Herman up, and had asked Mr. Pollock, of London, to look after the American end in London. The fight was for January, some seven months since I had last appeared in the ring against Patsy Wallace, and several months after I had decided to give up the game.

I remember the gleam in Ted Lewis's eyes when he came to see me.

" You'll accept, Jimmy ? "

" Oh, I don't know, Ted." I was not enthusiastic.

" But it's Herman—Pete Herman."

" Well——" I shrugged my shoulders. " If you're really keen."

So it happened, as quickly as that.

There was one thing I learned about after the fight that had nothing to do with the actual battle. A friend, J. H. Clifton, the sporting writer, let slip that he had wanted some seats for the Albert Hall and the cheapest was £3 10s. ! In the light of that, the purse was not so remarkable, after all. I cannot criticise the promoters.

Big fight tickets must go for what they can fetch. But £3 10s. does seem a bit thick, and when I remember the war-time story of Peggy Bettinson suffering agony while selling 2s. 6d. tickets at the old picture house— well, I hope I shall be forgiven a smile. But it seems a pity that the average fight-fan is often prevented by high prices from getting into the hall.

There were difficulties, for the Americans wanted terms we were not anxious to give. For instance, they demanded a twenty-round contest, a change from the usual American short-distance fight. I wanted fifteen rounds : 'Lisbeth and Lewis were with me.

But the bait was tempting.

Pollock went up to £8,000, with training expenses of £250, all of which was to be deposited in a London bank seven days before the fight. It was a colossal sum, while in addition there was my belief that I could beat Herman. I believed, and I still believe, that had the fight gone its normal way, I should have had the verdict, if not a knock-out.

But there is Fate as well as boxers to hit at champions.

I hope I do not sound as though I am grousing and preparing excuses in advance. Writing so long after the event any bitterness I might have felt has completely gone. But things certainly did not go right after the signing of that contract. It is true that I had some misgivings : twenty rounds, for an oldish boxer, was a long stretch : fifteen, I felt, was an ample test of ability. But we signed up for the twenty, with a weight of eight stone six pounds. My own weight, at the time, was seven stone one. Another irritating factor was the time for the weigh-in.

Before getting to that, however, we had learned

that the Prince of Wales was to be at the ringside. I was delighted, for His Royal Highness had always been a friendly patron of the sport and I was never likely to forget the fillip his summons to the *Renown* had given us before we left New York for Milwaukee.

Trouble descended like an avalanche.

The experienced boxer appreciates the importance of the weigh-in, and we understood that it would be just before the fight. When we reached the Hall, however, we learned that Herman had gone to the scales at two o'clock, and his manager—Sam Goldstein—showed articles of agreement to prove that this had been laid down as a condition.

Ted Lewis dashed out of the dressing-room for Rube Welch, and by that time I was feeling at a wicked nervous stretch. I had not been in the ring for seven months, remember, and for the most part my earlier fights had produced no disturbance just before the time for starting. At that moment my dressing-room was crowded; people were arguing and shouting at each other while I was getting ready, and I began to feel my head going round. I had already been tensed up to the limit. This was going past it.

And a subdued roar was coming from the crowd.

The fight was being delayed, while Battling Levinsky, with an injured hand, had been unable to fight Bombardier Billy Wells in a preliminary. That news had put the crowd in a bad temper, and the delay over the main fight of the evening was likely to cause a riot.

There was another, and justifiable, grievance from the spectators. In those early days of the news reel, it was not easy to get the lights working as well as they might do, and the film lights, covered with a wide canopy, hid the ring from the gallery and upper part of the balcony. Film or no film, that should never have been allowed.

All this kept percolating through to me, and I do not remember being on edge before a fight as I was that evening. I knew the Prince was waiting, with Lord Lonsdale and many other prominent folk. I hated the idea of letting them down, but Ted came back swearing he would not carry on. The whole trouble of course was that no one had scrutinised Herman's agreement to make sure that it was identical with mine.

" Well for heaven's sake ! " I remember protesting, " can't Herman weigh in again now ? What's to stop him ? "

Nothing, excepting that neither he nor Goldstein would agree ; obviously because he was well over the poundage. Many people were gate-crashing the dressing-rooms to find the cause of the hold-up and a dozen were hurling advice at me at the same time.

Then I lost my temper.

"I don't care what Herman thinks and says, I don't care about the money—I'm not letting the Prince and the crowd down. I'm going to fight Herman, I'm tired of these arguments." Or words to that effect.

I had hardly uttered them, and Ted had hardly started to protest, when Lord Lonsdale came in. In a short while the decision had been made and I was escorted to the ringside to meet the Prince yet again.

He smiled up at me cheerfully and as he shook hands I knew I could not have backed out.

" Do you think you can beat him ? " he asked.

I shook my head doubtfully.

"I'll do my best, Your Highness, but I don't

think so much of my chance after all this bother. But he will have to knock me senseless to win."

The Prince wished me good luck and I went through the ropes. I remember the tremendous hooting against Herman when he came through, but it probably worried him less than me. His dressing-room had been closely guarded, and he had been waiting alone with his seconds. His manager was absolutely right to do that. Our camp had been badly rattled, and we had suffered from it.

Herman was at least three pounds over weight: I would not state this boldly unless I were sure of my facts. It meant that I was giving away a stone and eight pounds against the finest bantam-weight fighter of the day. It was a handicap that it was simply crazy to accept.

Well it was done, crazy or not.

Before going on to the fight, there are two things of interest—first, the part the Prince of Wales played that night. While the crowd was getting hostile and threatening trouble, someone called out asking him for a speech. The Prince promptly stepped into the ring and, I was told afterwards, saved a dangerous situation by brief, well-turned phases that just caught the humour of the thousands present. He can judge men, singly or in crowds, superbly.

The other feature was an announcement from the ring which I insisted on the M.C. making. The fight was not under the weights advertised, Herman had too big an advantage for me to be really confident, and I had a request put out that all bets prior to the fight should be cancelled. It was a sufficient omen, I think, for most of those present.

★

HERMAN AND PANCHO VILLA

I DO NOT KNOW WHAT THE PUBLIC THOUGHT OF IT, but I have an idea of what they would have thought had Herman realised how near he was to finishing me in the second round. In the opening round we had simply tested each other: in the second he found a right to the chin that shook me.

Happily I managed to recover. I know we were both going very warily, but gradually I managed to get ahead on points. I think it was the ninth round when I just topped his total, and as far as I can recall, he did not catch me up again. On the other hand, Herman, playing a waiting game, let me establish the lead with a view to preserving his strength for a knock out.

The finish really came in the seventeenth round.

Instead of feinting with his left, as usual, Herman laid a trap and I walked into it. He caught me with a straight right to the chin that sent me reeling to the ropes, then through the middle strand. My head thudded on the edge of the ring, but I did not realise how seriously I had injured myself. I remember the referee, Jack Smith, saying:

" I've got to pick you up, Jimmy—you don't know the way to stay down."

232

And he tucked me under his arm and deposited me very gently in my seat.

This happened after I kept getting up and going down again, for Herman had me where he wanted me. I do not remember any pain in my head at the time, and I can say sincerely that Herman beat me because he was the better boxer; the best I had met. I do not think there was another bantam to touch him at that time.

His boxing was uncanny, with a defensive skill and anticipation almost incredible; a flashing attack that was world-beating. No other boxer, I think, had his genius. And I shall always be grieved that he suffered the worst thing a boxer could—a blindness that slowly incapacitated him until he was finally unable to see with either eye. That was, perhaps, the greatest tragedy of the ring.

Well, Herman had beaten me.

Seventeen rounds, in which I had had a severe battering and after which Peggy Bettinson said :

"You have been beaten by the greatest bantam of all time. He knows as much about boxing as Jim Driscoll, Packey McFarland and Jim Corbett. It's no disgrace to be beaten by such a perfect master. I must say you're extraordinary to have lasted seventeen rounds with him."

I often wish, now, that I had not.

The blow on the edge of the ring had caused concussion, and it was boxer's instinct that kept me going. The full effect of the blow was hardly revealed at the time, but I believe I would have been much fitter, after my boxing *finale*, had Herman knocked me out earlier in the bout. On the other hand, I would gladly risk the chance again if I could go back the years and relive the fight, without that absurd, astonishing bother before the duel.

I have tried to make it clear why Ted Lewis was so adamant about the weighing-in affair, which I believe upset my chance. Unless you can absolutely rely on the weights you are going to fight, it is impossible to train with that excess in mind. Three pounds is not much, but it is virtually thirty pounds when allied to a punch with the speed that Herman used.

That I hope will show the vital importance of three pounds as much as anything I could say : rhetoric and argument were never my strong points !

Ted was heart-broken (I speak almost literally) after the fight, and he reproached himself on two counts : on allowing the error to be possible, and on agreeing to take the fight over twenty rounds. For the most ironic fact that transpired after the battle was that I was well ahead of Herman on points to the fifteenth round. Against that, as I have said, Herman had deliberately given points away, believing he could finish with a knock-out. And from a bantam-weight of his superb skill, it is quite possible he would have won in any case.

Poor Pete. What a career he would have had if blindness had not overcome him, breaking across his boxing when he was only on the threshold of his career.

A little out of place, I would like to talk of another boxer who went blind. No one who knew him would class Alf Mansfield in quite the same category as Pete Herman, but Alf was a wonderful fighter ; no mean boxer, and a man with all the courage you could want in the ring. His trainer was Jack Goodwin, who had trained some of the finest English boys. As you already know, we had been matched twice, at Leeds and the Old West London Stadium.

Goodwin has called Mansfield my greatest rival, and while I cannot entirely subscribe to that opinion, he was certainly one of the most difficult fighters to beat, while without the trouble with his eyes he might have developed into a much better boxer than he did.

Naturally his camp kept the fact of the approaching blindness a careful secret. It was C. B. Cochran who had offered to stage our third fight (well before the U.S.A. trip) at the Holborn Stadium, and I was only too glad to put the gloves on with Alf again. There was another weigh-in problem there, for Alf, nearly undressed, turned the scale at eight stone four pounds, but Goodwin questioned the accuracy of the scales. In we marched to a Boots' (chemist) next door and Mansfield was several pounds lighter on it.

It was generally believed that Mansfield could not last ten rounds. I naturally hoped he would not, but I knew he had plenty of ability and courage. Actually he did extremely well, until—towards the end—I realised he was timing badly, and began to suspect something was the matter with his right eye. I did not know for a long time that it was entirely sightless.

Mansfield fell into an error of ring tactics. He was tiring towards the thirteenth round and I put him down with a fierce right. Instead of taking advantage of a long count, he was up again quickly. A tottering opponent after that, he was comparatively easy.

The Mansfield fight was of particular interest

because there was a clamour in England that I had gone back. I did not think so : actually Mansfield always made it difficult to fight at top stretch, and he could bring out some surprisingly clever tactics at times. At all events I had my most difficult fights, and the American tour, afterwards.

All of which comes out of place because Mansfield and Herman were to fall victims to blindness.

After the Herman fight, I decided for a second time to retire. Lonsdale (the house) held attractions that nothing else could do. My youngsters were getting to an interesting stage, while 'Lisbeth, despite her loyalty and continual presence, was hardly having the life a wife should expect. I had been boxing hard for twelve years and more and I thought, sincerely, that the Herman fight had been a warning that I would be unwise to carry on. Moreover, after the concussion that had followed the Herman affair I suffered a great deal of pain in the head.

Throughout the past twelve years my only " drink " had been the glass of champagne after a fight, and I had never touched a cigarette. I am still equally abstemious, but let me hasten to refute any suggestions of being a spoil-sport : the next man can smoke and drink as much as he likes, and I doubt whether it will do him any serious harm.

Back to Radyr again, then, and a gradual fading from the limelight. I was a long way from fit, although I would have spasms when I felt on top of the world. The friendliness of people was astonishing : I think I could have had a free dinner every night of the week, had I wanted it !

I did give an exhibition at Mountain Ash about that

time.   Warm-hearted Dai Evans promoted a show in aid of the miners during the 1921 strike, and I gladly offered to meet any two boys he cared to put up. The show was memorable because no one believed I would turn up.   Dai told me he was scoffed at for asking me.   There was a grand procession to the Pavilion, in which I played as insignificant part as possible, and it was grand to hear a real Welsh welcome at the ringside.   Ernie Robinson of Cwm and Billy Jones of Ynysddu put up a pleasant show with me (one at a time, of course).   I remember Dai's hot, smiling face when he announced a total subscription to the strikers' fund of £184 odd.   I auctioned my gloves for £12 10s.

Soon after came another big " bribe," for that was, in effect, what it amounted to.   The Americans badly wanted to see me over there again.   While I should have loved to go back, I had no desire for another tour : but the offer finally materialised into £13,000 for a single fight for the world championship, and it looked as though Frankie Genaro would be my opponent.

I forget how long it was before I accepted.

I know that I had a letter from O'Rourke one day telling me he had offered £8,000 for the match, and I dashed round to Ted Lewis.

" Here, what does this mean, man.   You've told me nothing."

" I didn't mean to," said Ted bluntly.   " You're retired, Jimmy, there's nothing else to it."

" I'm not so sure," said I.   " We'll see."

Actually I was attracted by the prospect, although I knew the value of Ted's judgment.   First one then another of my friends backed the suggestion and Ted was secretly anxious that I should go : much though he objected for my sake. He wanted more than anything else to have me retire on a winning note, and a fight in the States, against the acknowledged " second best " —if I dare say that at this stage—was the only one in which I could finish with a real blaze of glory. Yet he was afraid of the result.

Let me be honest. That idea of finishing in a blaze of glory attracted me. In fact, Lewis was the only one who stood out at the end.

I can see 'Lisbeth and Lewis arguing now, Lewis quiet-voiced ; his leonine head held downwards, with an occasional : " Eh, I can't hear ? " 'Lisbeth getting worked up : " He's going to fight, do you hear, he's going to fight. He wants to."

Finally Lewis gave in.

We travelled to the States in mid-summer this time, and I particularly remember playing golf with Robert Edgren, perhaps the most prominent sports writer in America, at a sun temperature of 130 degrees !

Was it hot !

And not only was it hot, but I had to put on a little weight, which seemed impossible. Lieutenant Alec Gallagher, of the New Jersey detective department, a large, jovial and enthusiastic fight fan, came in one day.

" What is it you're wanting, Jimmy ? "

" Flesh," said I. " Several pounds of it."

" Oh, it's a little extra weight, is it ? I know exactly the thing to do for you."

" How can I eat heavy stuff in this weather ; be sensible, man ! "

" Heavy stuff ! " roared Gallagher, " I'm suggesting ice-cream ! "

And ice-cream came, gallon after gallon, and I developed more than a liking for it, although it is hard to think of anything less calculated to be good for training. It did me no harm, nevertheless, and, although it put on little flesh, it made life cooler.

Instead of Genaro, the Philippine, Pancho Villa, was chosen to be my opponent. I was not perturbed by this decision, although I knew Villa had a reputation for tremendous fighting.

There was little of exceptional interest during training : everything was quite straight-forward. I played a great deal of golf at 130 degrees and had all the fuss made of me that I could possibly want.

It was rarely pointed out emphatically, however, that I had not fought in the ring since January 1921, and the Villa fight came in June 1923. That gap of two and a half years was important. I have said before that it robs a fighter of at least twenty per cent of his efficiency. Probably the percentage is higher with a boxer of nearly thirty-one, for the muscles begin to stiffen and no amount of sparring can bring out the speed necessary in the ring itself.

Which is by the way.

I remember seeing Villa in his corner. Dark, swarthy, a little round-shouldered, his slanting eyes summing me up, as mine were regarding him. He exuded confidence, but up to that moment I was equally confident. Blame it on to those eight-hundred odd fights, if you must : I did not think Pancho Villa would beat me.

I looked down at 'Lisbeth at the ringside. She was

with a well-known boxing critic, and I lifted a glove to them ; saw their return smile.

The gong went and Villa came like a tiger. He almost overwhelmed me in that first minute, but I knew his method of fighting and believed I could beat him. Villa slogged—there is no other word for it— and I kept him at a distance with a right and left, continually jabbing out. In the second round, and— as it proved—the vital one, he staggered me with a right to the chin. I fought back with all I knew, avoiding his rushes, keeping him off. I remember a tremendous left in the stomach that would have finished me had it landed ; it half-missed, and I countered with a right to the chin that jolted Villa badly.

The gong went.

I dropped my hands : I remember that clearly, and I also remember seeing something move in front of me. I did not realise what it was at the time. I do not remember the blow, but I am told that it sent me heavily to the canvas and brought the crowd to their feet with roars of disapproval. Apparently Benny Williams, my chief second, was more concerned with getting me round than claiming a foul.

They tell me they got me round, but I remember nothing about it. I do not remember going up for the third, fourth, fifth, sixth or seventh rounds. I do not recall being knocked out ; nor a single thing that happened until, one day three weeks afterwards, I found myself in a little seaside bungalow some distance from New York.

It is rather like sour grapes, I feel, to have an excuse for every time I lost a fight. Including the Sharkey bout and Pal Moore's, there were just five times when I failed to knock my man out or get the verdict, in a total of eight hundred and sixty-four fights. Many were of the old booth days, but they averaged one fight in every eight days of my fighting life.

I wonder whether I am justified in believing that, had I been entirely fit every time I entered the ring, not one of those verdicts would have been against me?

Well, it's of little odds now, but I sometimes feel about those fights much as I do when I miss an easy shot at snooker, or foozle a putt at the eighteenth: I could have won, but——

I have to fall back on 'Lisbeth again to tell what happened after the gong for the end of the second round. You will hardly need telling 'Lisbeth was at first indignant that the foul had not been declared, and that she hated to see me being knocked about the ring. She said afterwards:

" Villa fought like a wild-cat. He punched hard and viciously. Back-hand punches were his speciality, but every blow cut Jimmy to ribbons. Jimmy fought in a state of coma, although his hand seemed to respond to the working of his brain.

" Forty thousand people were there, and never was there a more orderly crowd. They were dumbstruck and fascinated. Nobody cheered. Everyone was glued to his seat. Why Villa was not disqualified for that foul punch cannot be explained. I say emphatically that the referee was lenient. But for it, another story might have been written. The majority of the ringside critics said it was a foul . . . and had somebody in Jimmy's corner been strong enough to insist on a foul Jimmy must have been given the verdict.

" When the big crowd began screaming : ' Stop it, stop it ! ' in the fifth round, I left my seat and went to wait for Jimmy in the dressing-room. Nothing would save him : I could not stop the fight, and I had to wait. I'm told that, amid tremendous shouting for the finish, cries of ' figue, figue ! ' from the Panay Islander's supporters— Jimmy took a left to the chin that sent him face downwards to the canvas ; out to the world."

It is 'Lisbeth who can tell you more of what happened afterwards than I can myself, for I was unconscious. Others said, too, that when the crowd thronged through the gates afterwards it was as if they were leaving a cemetery after a funeral, while there was hardly a cheer for the victor.

'Lisbeth, led into my dressing-room by a policeman, heard Al Thompson (whom we had met again over there) exclaim :

" He's blind, he's blind ! " Al immediately amended : " No, not Jimmy, of course, not Jimmy."

But it was.

'Lisbeth tells me that I looked like a mass of pulp as I was carried through, with a face as black as a negro's, eyes completely closed. There was Benny Williams applying ice to face and spine, Tom O'Rourke, the veteran manager who had brought me to the States, searching frantically for a doctor. But one of the most poignant moments must have been when Pancho Villa, the new champion, came to the table and, in his broken English, said :

" How—how you feel, Jimmy ? "

Then he recognised 'Lisbeth.

" You—his wife ? "

'Lisbeth nodded.

Villa pointed with a trembling finger at me, and muttered :

" Me no want to hurt him. Not me do that." And he turned and went, with the tears streaming down his face. An odd sight that must have been. 'Lisbeth believes that he tried to tell her that he fought on orders, and not entirely of his own free will.

Poor Villa. He died not long afterwards, and he gained a lot of notoriety after that foul blow. But what did it amount to, after all ? I had been hit before, after the gong : it was the result, not the cause, that made it a sensation. In the excitement it is not always easy for a man to hear the gong : at times they are not as loud as they should be. If there was a fault, it was the referee's, and probably had he thought the foul deliberate, he would have stopped the fight then.

But if he made a real mistake, it was in allowing the fight to continue. How often have I wished that fights could be stopped to prevent the other man being hit so badly ? But the human element is not reliable, and after all, they thought I could recover and come back.

'Lisbeth tells me that O'Rourke eventually returned with a big man (Dr. Lois Draper, one-time college champion, and a famous osteopath) who reassured her promptly. He sat on the table like a tailor at work : in his own words :

" . . . the punches had jammed the neck and facial muscles, temporarily locked the neck to the spine, and produced a form of neurasthenia."

Four hours later 'Lisbeth saw him kneading at my neck, against his big body and she was growing more and more certain that I was dying. She must have been near hysteria, pleading with them to let me die peacefully. I'm glad I could not see or hear that! And then, apparently, Draper—bathed in perspiration and nearly exhausted—said: "Keep shouting ' Jimmy '! Keep shouting . . ."

'Lisbeth had ice in her hands, ice in her mouth, which had started to bleed badly as she cried and shouted. What a scene it must have been!

As I have said, I had no recollection of coming round, and 'Lisbeth told me afterwards that when we got back to New Jersey we were besieged by reporters and others and there was no chance of real peace. Luckily for her Frankie Burns, the bantam-weight champion, and his wife were close by. They had a bungalow on a small island near New York, and insisted on taking us there until I was reasonably fit again.

In order to avoid the crowd we went over in a small boat. But the heavens were as unkind as the unwanted visitors, for a thunderstorm broke.

'Lisbeth says none of them expected to reach land.

When the boat was within easy distance a lightning flash struck two men standing on the small landing-stage. Both were killed instantaneously.

In that horror, then, they got me ashore, spoon-fed me with milk and ice-cream, and finally, after three weeks, I recognised 'Lisbeth. Burns and his wife were a wonderful pair of friends throughout the aftermath of that Villa fight.

The crisis was past.

It was the eclipse of my fighting days : but for Draper and 'Lisbeth it would probably have been the eclipse in more ways than one, but——

Just after ten years later, Bob Edgren, writing in the *San Francisco Chronicle*, gave his well-considered opinion of the fight, thus :

" The nearest thing to a killing that wasn't quite a killing was in the Wilde-Villa fight for the world's fly-weight championship. Champion Wilde had been brought over from England to fight Villa, who had knocked out Johnny Buff for the American title.

" WHEN VILLA FOULED LITTLE ENGLISH BOXER

" Wilde started deliberately and Villa forced the fighting. They were mixing fast when the bell rang ending the second round. Wilde dropped his hands and partly turned to go to his corner. Pancho had drawn his right hand back for a swing. I saw him stop and hold back the blow for an instant. But there was Wilde hands down, head turned away, in easy range. Either the temptation was too great or instinct too strong. Villa let the swing go with everything behind it, landing square on Wilde's chin.

" Relaxed and defenceless, Wilde was knocked cold. Seconds dragged him to his corner, worked over him nearly a minute before he stirred. They protested to the referee, but either Haley had turned at the bell and didn't see the foul punch or he figured Villa had it started when the bell rang. Can't figure it any other way, for Haley is square.

Patsy ignored the protests. The bell rang again. Wilde's seconds lifted him to his feet and pushed him from the corner. He staggered toward Villa.

" Wilde could hardly lift his hands and only instinct kept him reeling about and trying to fight back while Villa slugged furiously in an effort to finish him. It was sheer slaughter, but the foul blow after the bell had been passed by, Wilde was still on his feet, and it is one of the pleasant customs of the ring to let a champion take his beating until he drops.

" Crowd got Thrills but Wilde took Beating

" Wilde was terribly beaten and was terribly knocked out in the seventh round. He was carried unconscious to the dressing-room and was in a coma for hours after the fight. In fact, I was told afterwards that it was not until two in the morning that the doctors decided he'd live.

" Having been in a good position to see Villa's action it was my opinion that the blow was un-questionably foul and that Villa should have been disqualified at once, and Wilde never should have been allowed to go on after being so badly knocked out by a foul blow that he had no possible chance to recover, whether the ending after the second round was a disappointment to the crowd or not."

And so the end of the game.
But was it the end ?
Of my actual fighting days, of course, but I have never lost touch with the ring, and I hope I never shall. In the fifteen years since that American finale,

I have seen many things, lost a great deal of money, made a little, but generally enjoyed retirement, even if the itch to fight has often been in my hands. Yet I have never put the gloves on since, chiefly because of Sir Alfred Fripp's warning :

" You'll kill yourself if you do, Mr. Wilde."

Well, I feel as fit as ever, and presumably I've looked after myself (or 'Lisbeth has !).

But shall we have a look at the money-and-boxing problem ?

★

MONEY AND BOXING

I OFTEN WISH I HAD BEEN A FINANCIAL WIZARD, as well as useful with my fists. I could also say I wish I had been born ten years later, so that I would have been in time to fight practically all my important contests during the big-money days of modern fighting. In view of the last dozen or so fights that I had, I could hardly complain of my earning powers, although it must not be thought—it frequently is— that if a boxer gets a purse of £10,000 he is that amount in pocket.

What are the charges on a first-class boxer?

They remain more or less steady, apart from the fluctuating Income Tax figures (and the less said about that the better: puzzling out Income Tax statements has given me far more anxiety than brooding over any coming opponent). The usual charge for a manager is twenty-five per cent, bringing the £10,000 down to £7500. (My arithmetic, I feel, is improving.) Allow at least £500 for various fees during training, and after the fight. Here is a rough summary of the way the money goes :

Trainer	. . .	£75	o	o
Sparring partners	.	125	o	o
Camp food .	. .	75	o	o
Equipment .	. .	50	o	o
Train fares, etc.	.	25	o	o
Hotel expenses	.	50	o	o
Tips and general	.	100	o	o
		£500	o	o

The figures are liable to vary considerably either way, but I can easily imagine a great number of people questioning the necessity of such expenditure, particularly when a boxer has to get just as fit, very often, on a fight that will not earn him more than a few hundred pounds. With the spotlight of publicity, however, expenses go shooting up. That is not peculiar to boxing. Give a man who has been managing to jog along on £250 a year a sudden income of a thousand a year, and it is reasonably certain that he will find it just as difficult to spin his extra money out to meet the extra obligations that, in some queer but almost inevitable way, make themselves felt.

Let me analyse the figures, then, for a big fight.

The strict training will often cover a period of several months, and it must be remembered that the trainer has to be paid over a twelve-month period (or whatever is contracted). With my Herman bout, for instance, trainer's fees were considerably heavier than £75 because it was my only fight for a long time. Sparring partners are sometimes hired by the week, say £3 to £5 weekly, *plus* a present after the fight. (This is accepted practice, and does not rank for Income Tax, either way!) Others get ten shillings or a pound for each time they appear in the ring, and it can easily be seen that five sparring partners at five pounds a week for five weeks makes the £125 I have allowed, without the presents, which are included in the " tips and general " item.

In the camp, too, are the sparring partners, trainer, occasionally supplementary boys and, not unnaturally, the boxer. None has poor food, and none of them is a poor eater. It is nothing to have a meat bill, during training, for fifty or sixty pounds, and I fancy my estimate of £75 errs on the side of insufficiency. Frequently there are other expenses, but as I often (in fact practically always) trained at home, and 'Lisbeth did the cooking, I saved a great deal on them.

The same little army has to travel to the venue of the fight, and a championship boxer can hardly travel third class. The same number of people have to be looked after in London or the fight venue, usually for several days. Again I think the allowed hotel expense figure is too low, but it can stand as an average.

The £10,000, then, has already shrunk to £7000, before our Income Tax collector comes along for his share of round about ten shillings in the pound. Surtax has varied a great deal from year to year but it is a reasonable working figure. And so the net profit is just under four thousand pounds and four thousand pounds does not go as far as it might. The expenses of keeping up appearances are something it is extremely difficult to compute, and the one vital factor is that the successful boxer must be a good fellow.

I know there will be arguments against that contention, but I believe it sincerely. It should be remembered that the atmosphere of the average training camp is one of good-fellowship and *camaraderie*, that an unpopular member of the camp rarely lasts there long, and that in training the quality of a man's technique is no more important than the quality of his smile. A medium-class sparring partner, for instance, is far better if he can be relied on to be cheerful throughout training, than a first-class man who is morose. It remains a fact that most good boxers are good fellows. The whys and wherefores are not so hard to discover, after all.

If a man can lose well, he is three parts of the way to being a pleasant companion. If he can't lose well, he is nine-tenths of the way out of the fight game. It's as simple as that. The odds on finding the temperament you need for training are, therefore, considerable.

But there is more to that good-fellow business than being hail-fellow-well-met with your own particular little crowd, or with the boxing circle itself. Let me try and give an idea, for instance, of the calls on one's time (more to-day, perhaps, than in my day, apart from the war-period activities).

I'm not suggesting that the calls I am listing would come on a single day, or in any one week, but they are liable to come between one fight and another, or between one money-earning day and the next.

The morning post brings a note something like this:

" DEAR JIMMY,

" Everyone down here is delighted to know you beat So-and-so last week, and hopes to see you here again before long. As a matter of fact we are promoting a boxing night, in three weeks' time, on behalf of such-and-such a cause. If you could give an exhibition it would prove a tremendous draw. Please do try.

" Yours sincerely,

" . . . "

Unless one has a particularly important engagement on the date, one has to go. The " here " represents a populous part of the country, where your reputation is good and must be maintained—apart from the genuine interest in the cause : it is always a commendable one. It is for charity, and although expenses will be offered, they can hardly be accepted (that rules, at least, in the boxing world). Fares and hotel frequently take thirty or forty pounds.

Then you will be walking along Fleet Street, and meet a sports writer, whom you automatically take to the nearest place for a drink and a chat, during which he says :

" By the way, Jimmy, I'd be awfully glad if you'll come to the paper's Annual Dinner and Dance. Are you free on the seventeenth."

" Yes, I think so."

" Good man. Bring Mrs. Wilde, of course."

" She'll like it, I'm sure."

So it is fixed, and I am genuinely glad to go ; but anyone who thinks that an evening at that Dinner and Dance is a cheap one is making a wrong guess. And it is not only one night. Such invitations are continuous. A reunion dinner here : a dinner for a touring team of footballers or cricketers, a boxing tournament for some minor charity, a benefit night for a man who has fallen on hard times—they are countless. For my own part, and I think I speak for practically every well-known boxer, life would not be complete without them. We go, gladly; we enjoy ourselves, we haven't a single regret, but over a year we are several hundred pounds out of pocket.

I won't say much about the number of fivers that are " lent " in the course of a year !

Then there is the other side of the picture. The late Sir Harry Preston's shows on behalf of the Royal Sussex Hospital, Brighton, were wonderfully well-managed, and that grand sportsman made sure that anyone who helped him was not out of pocket. But for every promoter of such charities who could and did cover expenses out of his own pocket, there are dozens who simply cannot afford to. The charity is no less deserving, though. Again, there will be a telephone call from (let us say) Mr. Cochran.

" That you, Jimmy."

" Why yes, who is that ? "

" C. B. Cochran here. Jimmy, I could use you for such-and-such a show, if you'd care to join the party. A week, say, from . . ."

" Yes, I'm free, I'll be glad to."

And it will be fixed. The payment for this comparatively easy stage-turn is excellent, but it comes very rarely. In recent years, and long after I had finished with boxing, I have appeared in *In Town To-night* at various variety houses with Jack Bloomfield as compère, and in company with Billy Wells, Dave Crowley (a promising youngster, Dave, watch him[1]) and others, and it all helps to keep the money coming in, as well as going out.

[1] Since I wrote this, Dave has won the English light-weight championship.

In parenthesis, Jack makes a fine compère, and he must be one of the best known figures in the West End, for practically everyone visits his Bear Street Hotel sooner or later.

I think I have said enough about the expenses, normal and unexpected, that continually crop up, and I hope I have made it convincing that a boxer does not get £10,000 should he gain a £10,000 purse.

There is another aspect of the picture, however.

To take a particular example, there was my own American tour and the few fights immediately before and after it. Perhaps the best way of showing the advantages of such a tour will be to list the fights and the purses. (I can almost hear the envious sighs of many who see that I earned over two thousand pounds for one round with Bobby Dyson.)

Date.	Opponent.	Result.			Purse.
July 17, 1919	Pal Moore	20 Rounds	W.O.P.		£5,000
Dec. 6, 1919	Sharkey	No decision			$10,000
Jan. 8, 1920	Johnny Asher	8 Rounds, N.D.			£8,000
Jan. 29, 1920	Mike Ertle	3	do.	K.O.	$10,000
Feb. 19, 1920	Russell	7	do.	K.O.	$10,000
March 3, 1920	Wallace	6	do.	N.D.	$8,000
March 11, 1920	Mason	12	do.	N.D.	$10,000
April 12, 1920	Zulu Kid	10	do.	N.D.	$8,000
April 21, 1920	Bat Murray	8	do.	K.O.	$6,000
May 1, 1920	Dyson	1	do.	K.O.	$10,000
May 13, 1920	Murray	2	do.	K.O.	$6,000
May 24, 1920	Wallace	10	do.	N.D.	$8,000
Jan. 13, 1921	Herman	17	do.	Lost	£8,000
June 18, 1923	Villa	7	do.	Lost	£13,000

N.D.   No Decision contest.
K.O.   Knock Out.
W.O.P. Won on points.

Calling the dollar worth four to a pound, it will be seen that the 1919–1920 tour netted some £23,500. *But*, there was American Income Tax and then English Income Tax. There were colossal expenses, apart from those incurred while training, for we were a party of four throughout the trip. It must have cost £2000. And, ironically, the table shows that the two last fights, which I lost, brought me practically as much as the whole American tour.

Prior to the War big-fight money was comparatively small. A purse of £500 was a big one, and only once before the War, I think, did I get more than four figures. Until the Pal Moore fight, my biggest purse was with Joe Conn, at Stamford Bridge, worth altogether (save the authorities !) £2000, a great deal of which was paid in diamonds, you will remember.

I see no object in trying to trace the money I received from each fight ; which is as well, because I have no record of them all, unfortunately. It seems sufficient to say that when at last I retired (for the third time, remember, and when I was suffering from loss of memory after the Pancho Villa bout) I had something like £70,000, which still seems a lot of money.

For some years I did very little The late Sir Alfred Fripp saw me soon after I returned to England. I was fit enough in myself, but my mind was often a complete blank where memory was concerned, and I could hardly remember what I had said from one sentence to the next. Sir Alfred examined me at length, and then said :

" Do you drink, Mr. Wilde ? "

" An occasional glass of wine, that's all."

" Best to cut it all out, you'll find. There's a clot of blood circulating and it might—in fact I think it will—work away. But you'll have to go very carefully, and you must not take alcohol."

" And you think I'll be all right ? "

" Yes, with care, and in time."

That was at least hopeful, although it did not rob the situation of its irony. I was a comparatively wealthy man ; for the first time in my life I had leisure to enjoy wealth : and I had to be treated like a semi-invalid. The process of recovery was slow. I think I am reasonably fit to-day, but, as I have said, I have never dared to put the gloves on again, no matter how mild a competition might be. On the other hand, I am much fitter than I was ten and fifteen years ago.

I was able to do a bit, one way and the other. I ventured into several speculations, none of which could be called profitable. A Starting-Price business in Cardiff prospered for a time, but eventually went under, with a net loss of some ten thousand pounds. Let me confess, I lost a bit on betting, too. I bought several cinemas in South Wales, including the Coliseum at Tylorstown where I won that melting coffee set, but the depression in the Rhondda Valley saw the value of the houses slump almost to nothing. They are picking up, slowly, and now represent a useful income, but the loss was considerable. These business losses ran at the same time as the expensive education of my two boys at King's College, Taunton, and other expenses which, I found, were practically as high in retirement as they had been in the heyday of my boxing.

It was in co-operation with poor Jimmy White that I lost most heavily however.

Jimmy had been a great patron of boxing, and I was proud to associate myself with him in anything. 'Lisbeth, let me say at once, was always urging me to be more cautious with my dealings with Jimmy as a financier. I don't know whether she had a gift of second sight; whether it was that old friend, feminine intuition, or whether it was simple ca'canniness, if I dare say that of a Welsh woman. At all events, we had some grand arguments about the investment in *Katja the Dancer*, at Daly's.

That show, some of you will remember, was running when Jimmy White committed suicide. The details of my own investment, of well over ten thousand pounds, made me shudder to contemplate, even eleven years afterwards.

I had put up some money on Jimmy White's assurance that the show would be a big success but, of course, with no idea of his financial difficulties. At the time I was living at Radyr, with the S.P. business staggering a little in Cardiff. Some weeks afterwards 'Lisbeth grew more and more worried about my investments with White. We had some fierce arguments, I convinced there was nothing to worry about, and 'Lisbeth scared of something she could not really explain. Then White suggested I put more into *Katja*.

In the first place 'Lisbeth did not want me to invest anything in the show, and we came close to a serious quarrel. Finally, I went to the safe to get out the shares for realising and investing. 'Lisbeth followed me.

" You won't do it, do you hear ? "

" Whose money is it, I ask you ? "

" Mine as much as yours. Give me them ! "

We had a struggle for the shares, some of which were actually torn before I got them. 'Lisbeth was furious.

" I've warned you. You've lost enough already. If you lose that, I've finished with you."

" Oh, nonsense, it's as safe with Jimmy White as any man."

Finally the investment was made, but when nothing in the way of returns promised, 'Lisbeth's fears grew stronger and our arguments started again.

" Ask him for it back," said 'Lisbeth. " Tell him you've had losses, and you must have it."

" No, I can't do that. The money's all right, I tell you."

" And I say it isn't, Jimmy ! Listen, will you tell him you want a thousand pounds quickly and see whether you get it ? "

" All right," said I, and we left for London that afternoon.

In my previous dealings with Jimmy White I had been more or less welcome every time I called at his offices. They rarely troubled to announce me and I just went in. But on that visit things were very different.

I called six days in succession, but was always put off. I knew Jimmy was in London, and at the office, but he was either at a conference, had just been called out, or was indisposed.

" I knew it," 'Lisbeth said daily. " I felt it. You must get your money back. Jimmy. Keep at him."

The seventh day was more successful.

I was shown into the financier's office, and Jimmy was full of apologies.

" I've had a dreadful week, Jimmy, and you've been deucedly unlucky. But I'm free at last—what can I do for you ? "

" Well," said I, a little awkwardly, for I was convinced by his manner that there was nothing to worry about, " I've run short of ready money. Can you let me have a thousand ? "

" Why, of course," he wrote the cheque out there and then and I returned in triumph to 'Lisbeth, whose doubts were silenced effectively. Cheered and quite confident again, and remembering White's assurances, I had nothing to worry about.

" There's a fortune in *Katja the Dancer*," he had assured me. " You'll be sitting absolutely pretty, Jimmy."

But two months went by with nothing more than hope and, on 'Lisbeth's suggestion, I asked for and obtained another thousand pounds.

It was only a few days afterwards that I entered the offices of the S.P. business to find 'Lisbeth with Bill Collis, my manager, there.

Both of them were looking white and worried, but I had no inkling of the coming news.

" Hello, 'Lisbeth, I didn't expect you."

" Have you seen the placards ? " 'Lisbeth demanded.

" Placards ? Why, no, what's on them ? "

Collis tried to say something, but 'Lisbeth broke in quickly.

" Jimmy White's committed suicide. Do you hear that ? "

Jimmy White—suicide !

I looked from one to the other. I remembered the talk with him, his assurances of a fortune, the fact that most of my available capital was tied up in the *Katja the Dancer* show.

" He's—done what ? " I asked stupidly.

" Killed himself," 'Lisbeth snapped. " I've told you and warned you. You've lost your money, and I'm leaving you ! "

I kept staring. Suicide. Suicide !

" And I'm leaving you ! " 'Lisbeth shouted again. The words forced themselves through my numbed mind, and I heard Collis say :

" You mustn't talk like that, Mrs. Wilde. It's a wicked thing to say ! "

" He's asked for it," stormed 'Lisbeth, and marched out of the office, with a scared Collis on her heels. Afterwards I learned that Collis had been remonstrating wildly, and 'Lisbeth had stopped him quickly, saying :

" Will you let me handle my husband my own way ? "

I was not conscious of being handled any way, but 'Lisbeth's words had started me thinking furiously, and when they came back, I began to argue. Gradually I " won " 'Lisbeth round, until she turned to Chella, the secretary.

" Go and get me a hundred pounds, Mr. Chella."

Money could be relied on to make me think just then.

" For what ? "

" We're going to London and we're going to have a good time," 'Lisbeth said, and shouted down my protests that we could not afford it. We had to afford it, she said, and the money was brought round. Within a few hours we were in London, and every night for a week we went to some show or other; she would give me no time to think, no peace at all. I think— and others have agreed—that if 'Lisbeth had not acted like that it would have broken me finally. As it is —well, the failure of the S.P. business and the continued slump in the picture-houses did not seem as important as they were, and we kept smiling.

Well, that was how the money was earned: and how a great deal of it was lost. Until 1923 boxing had been my business: my activities outside it had been disastrous, and so I decided to get back to it again. That, briefly, is why boxing is still my business, as apart from my chief interest in life.

★

GLIMPSES BEHIND THE SCENES

SEEING THAT THE BOOK IS NEARLY ALL " BEHIND THE scenes " of big boxing, this chapter heading needs explaining. The explanation is simple. It was my good fortune to be born with a love for boxing, and an ability above the average to exploit the fight game. But there are thousands of boys, loving the sport as much as I do, who spend their early days at it, earn as little as a pound for a fight of six rounds and, when it is realised that they have not the making of champions, local or national, they fall away, forgotten, often disfigured, always disheartened. The undertow of boxing. What happens to them ? How do they live, before and after their careers ?

I am afraid it is not a happy topic. My one reason for introducing it into these memoirs is a sincere feeling that until many of the conditions in boxing are altered, it will be the ruin more than the makings of many promising youngsters and—equally important from a different motive—English boxing will compare badly with that of the United States.

I have mentioned before that boxing in the States is over-controlled. The different States have varying rules. There is no central governing body, but each State has something in common with its fellows, and that :the public gymnasium system, where training is conducted. On payment of a reasonable fee youngsters with boxing ambition can get a try-out. If they show promise they can be sure of being supported, handled by an efficient manager, boosted— perhaps far above their true value, but none the less beneficially for them financially—trained by experts and given every chance of keeping fit.

Out of these gymnasia, which are really off-shoots of the old boxing booths, come the champions of America : too frequently, these days, the champions of the world. They are carefully picked ; go through a gruelling training and are matched against good men. They have to fight hard to get near the top, which they cannot reach without serious claims to first-rate technique and fighting courage.

There is an undertow in the States as well as over here, but unofficial managers are frowned on and the faults are not so glaringly apparent as in this country. Oddly enough, unofficial managers are frowned on more over here, perhaps, than in the States : but a large number of managers in England know too little about boxing. Their interest is personal and financial : they have little or no love of the game, which would fail to attract them but for the money-interest. Consequently more and more managers with the interest of boxing at heart are forced, by this competition, to adopt methods of which they certainly do not approve.

The methods are briefly these. A manager has on his books (usually tied to him by contracts signed in the late teens) anything from thirty to sixty " boys " of various weights. Matches are made, the fighting is poor, but each boxer earns a few shillings weekly for his manager. The manager makes a fair living, but the boxer, if he depends on fighting alone, is perilously close to starvation. To-day, happily, the conditions have improved and the minimum fighting terms established by the N.B.A. are :

		Winner.	*Loser.*
For 6 rounds	. .	£1 5s.	£1
„ 8 „	. .	£1 15s.	£1 10s.
„ 10 „	. .	£3	£2 10s.

I know what you are going to say. In your mind's eye is a picture of the list of the purses for my own fights, and the comparison is going to make you laugh. The figures are incredibly low : but they are accurate, and until a few months ago they were not enforced. Lower " fees " were frequently in operation.

It is not difficult to imagine the lives of young boys who, when they are lucky enough to get a fight, earn as little as the fixed minimum. Many of them are half-starved—literally, I'm afraid. Promising youngsters with no other income are forced into accepting tips, making absurd matches, being knocked about in the ring or at " training " and, in the early twenties, are no use for boxing. They are little enough use anywhere else, and they fade out completely.

How is it to be avoided ?

The one way is perhaps a hard one. Only boys with exceptional promise should be taken in hand by managers, while the others should be barred from appearing in public contests. No manager can hope to look after fifty or sixty youngsters, but he can handle five or six successfully. If this were the ruling practice the quality of the boys would be higher ; the crowds, and thus the gate-money, would increase, and conditions would improve both for the patron and the boxer himself. Moreover it would practically ensure that only boxers of old standing, or men with a long experience of the art, would become managers.

It is not my intention, in these memoirs, to break a lance with anyone. All I want to do is to appeal earnestly to all who are interested in boxing from any point of view to do their utmost to alter some of the prevailing conditions.

It has been my privilege to be President of the National Union of Boxers (now known as the National Boxing Association) since its foundation in 1935. The aims are sincere : the only central objective, in fact, is an improvement of boxing conditions. We are happy in the support of influential patrons, such as the Marquess of Queensberry and Sir Noel Curtis-Bennett, the Press, and many ruling champions. I believe the day will come when the N.B.A. and the British Boxing Board of Control will see eye to eye, and it will be a red-letter day in British boxing when their differences have been settled and they work amicably together.

It was only a week ago that representatives of the N.B.A. agreed to set up a board which would rank the six leading men in each of the eight weights. With such a ranking, the situation at the head of the table will be considerably clearer, and in yet another way boxing will owe a debt to the sporting writers, who were sent lists and asked to rank the boxers. I will mention none of them by name. The big names and the " special correspondents " all did their bit and deserve warm thanks. And as far as I can, I offer it.

Another aim at the moment is to prevent youngsters of twenty and under fighting fifteen rounds for a championship. The younger boys have not matured ; their muscles are not set, and when opposed to men of longer experience and greater endurance they get set back badly, perhaps irretrievably. Twelve rounds, I feel, is the limit they should go to ; many a comparatively unknown boxer would have been famous had he fought only six or eight rounds in his teens.

I was asked a few days ago what were the duties of a second. They are clear cut, if sometimes somewhat misunderstood. A good second can turn a losing fight into a winning one, and the importance of having an efficient man in your corner cannot be over-estimated. Jim Driscoll was the ideal man for it. He missed nothing and was always ready with advice at the end of a round. As though he were with me now I can hear him saying :

" You're doing all right, Jimmy. Try your left a bit more to his chin. And don't hurry, there's no hurry." Or, when I was inclined to mix it a little too early in the fight :

" Keep you back a bit, Jimmy, have a bit to spare ! "

And there, in a nutshell, is the value of a second. If he can help you—and watching the fight from the corner, but with a cooler mind than the boxers, he should know what is wanted—by pointing out how you can best wear your opponent down, or where you will find his weakness, he has done his job. Jim was quiet, knowing he had no official standing. It wasn't his job to bellow at you or anyone, but to keep you going, and make sure you spent the least possible energy while gaining points.

A second will be with you in training. He will know your weaknesses, help you to correct them, and in any case defend you from them in the ring itself. A good second can make a boxer better ; a poor one can ruin him. On the whole, I think they do a difficult job well.

★

THINGS FORGOTTEN

I AM AFRAID THAT AFTER THIS BOOK IS PUBLISHED I shall remember a host of things I have forgotten while writing it, apart from those last minute rushes to squeeze a little something in before the final proofs are passed. I don't know whether the average man finds it difficult to remember details over a period of twenty years and more. I offer at once both the excuse and apology that my memory has been faulty for a long time, chiefly because of that last fight in America. A great many people have helped me to recall various incidents that appeared worth relating, and 'Lisbeth has been a wonderful stand-by. One of the things I have remembered for myself, however, is that 'Lisbeth often used to sing at the Sir Harry Preston Charity Shows at Brighton, and brought the house down. Singing is inbred in most Welsh people. Like the vast majority, 'Lisbeth has had no training, but she provided an excellent turn for those memorable days.

Year after year I went down to Brighton for Sir Harry. Once I remember travelling down with the late Bertram Mills, who was on the Committee. What an astonishing man he was! It was always safe to rely on anything he said, and he was an organiser in a thousand. The most notable thing I remember about him, however, was his decisiveness. There was no hesitating, or beating about the bush. He answered every question with a definite " yes " or " no," and yet he never looked like causing any offence. I sometimes wonder whether I might have appeared with any success in his circus ? But perhaps it was as well that it was never put to the test. I did go to Epsom once in his famous coach and it took me back in memory to my first scarifying trip in a hansom cab. The traffic gave way to the Mills coach, though.

At one of the Brighton shows I boxed an exhibition with Carpentier again, which met with the almost inevitable success of exhibitions. He had a straight right that was as devastating as it was rare in a heavyweight boxer.

Sir Harry, who was always to be seen at the ringside of the N.S.C., had a characteristic way of greeting his friends.

Out would shoot his right hand and his smile would widen.

" How are you, Jimmy ? "

And as he took your hand he would pull you towards him, with a grip that was surprisingly powerful. He put 'Lisbeth and me up at the Royal Albion, for most of the shows, and with him and Lady Preston we had many enjoyable days.

He had the patronage of the Prince of Wales and the Duke of York for those shows at the Dome (on behalf of the Royal Sussex County Hospital), and certainly the Kings of the Ring. Tommy Burns, Pat o'Keeffe, Dick Smith, Matt Wells, Joe Bowker (to whom amateur boxing owes a great debt),

Carpentier, Dempsey, Moran, Beckett—names without number. The amateurs were often represented, and particularly do I remember the then amateur world heavy-weight champion, the late Captain Ernest Chandler ; the one-legged Major Micky Leahy, and Mr. Eddie Egan. Bombardier Billy Wells was often there—once after Carpentier had knocked him out on the previous night—Phil Scott, Boy McCormick, a myriad others. Tom Webster usually drew the cartoons for the programme.

I once boxed Steve Donoghue in a " funny " bout that brought the house down. Across Steve's sweater was " Donoghue Up ! " and in his corner was Tom Webster.

Between rounds Tom rushed in, collected Steve, and started scrubbing his teeth with a tooth-paste that foamed like white clouds. There was Steve, spluttering but helpless, and Tom working like a second fearful that his man was fated to lose.

How fond fighting men were of Sir Harry ! Dempsey once put off urgent business (at the end of his honeymoon tour) to stay to box at Brighton because he had promised, and his wife, Estelle Taylor —tired of England's climate and unwell—cheerfully waited with him. Carpentier put himself out to be present, and it was before one show we exchanged notes on our humbler days, with an interested audience. Georges started it, telling us that he had once earned a few francs a week as a messenger for a bum-bailiff of Lens. And Descamps held us fascinated by his experiences as a mesmerist, thought-reader and conjurer on the halls, and a Professor of English boxing !

The Royal Sussex County Hospital benefited by some £40,000 from Sir Harry Preston's shows, while several thousand were given to other hospitals. The money was not earned only by the boxing, though. At the first show Sir Walter de Frece conducted a grand auction.

" Here," he declared, " is the real fight of the evening. On my left Benevolence, and on my right Suffering and Want ! "

Mr. Bernhard Baron (his career as romantic as Carpentier's) once contributed generously; Sir Edward Marshall Hall sent a large contribution from the Rothschild Trust; Sir Alfred Fripp from the fund of the Royal and Ancient Order of Frothblowers, and others came from men and women from every sphere. There could be no greater tribute to Sir Harry's magnetic personality or his capacity for hard work.

I have always been happy to help at charity shows, and during the War in particular my services were in considerable demand. Sportsmen as a whole do a great deal of it ; perhaps we realise that it is a tribute to our popularity. I remember only a year or two back going to Margate for a show on behalf of the local hospital. Among many others present was Alex James, that wizard of the football field who is as entertaining in private life as he is—unhappily I should say " was " now he has retired—in public. Mr. George Allison, the Arsenal manager, was with us too.

Another time I went to a Boys' Club effort at Harrogate, and collected twenty pounds after some strenuous talking and a great display of the Lonsdale

Belt, my proudest possession. I shall never cease being grateful to whoever suggested taking the belt as a money-making side-show, for the next morning I had a telephone call from David, in my London flat.

David had been out until late the previous night and, coming home, had noticed a muddle in the rooms but put it down to me. (I am not the tidiest of people!) In the morning he looked more carefully, missed a number of cups and prizes from their cabinet, and wanted to know whether I had taken them with me.

" Taken them ? No, I've only got the belt, why ? "

" Well, someone has," said David.

'Lisbeth and I raced back to Golders Green to find the police in possession. Of the one hundred and fifty trophies I had collected and prized, twenty-three of the best were gone. So was a small cup that Verdun had won in a marathon race at King's College, Taunton, and 'Lisbeth was far more upset about this than the others. Nothing was returned despite our appeal, and the camera-work and general investigation of the police.

The value of the trophies to the thief or thieves must have been very little. They were all silver, and worth only a melting price. Yet the sentimental value to us was considerable.

I would like five minutes alone with that light-fingered gentleman, fighting under any conditions he likes.

Enthusiasm for any sport or cause always cheers me, and the keenness of the boys at Harrogate made up to some degree for my losses. Another boys' movement in which I have been interested for a long time is the Boy Scouts' organisation. I have always found it surprising how the Scouts try to live up to the strict code imposed on them, and I had some great fun, one week, when I was with Viscount Castlereagh at a Sunderland camp for Scouts. His enthusiasm for this movement is at least equal to his keenness for boxing, and his personality is so charming that when he has said rather ruefully that one of his big regrets is that he did not see me in action in the ring I feel tempted to don the gloves again.

A few days ago I was happy to have this letter :

" My dear Jimmy,

      " I am very glad indeed to hear that you are publishing a book dealing with your remarkable career. Much has already been written about you, but I feel that a book of this type is long overdue. You will go down to history not merely as the most remarkable exponent of the art that any country has produced, but also as one of the greatest sportsmen in the game.

      " It is one of my chief regrets that I never saw you in action in the ring, but I have been associated with you in something far greater than your championship triumphs. You always used your great reputation and your good name to help any good cause or movement. I remember year after year, meeting you in Sunderland at the dinner preceding the Boy Scouts' Boxing Tournament, at which you were the third man in the ring. You came all the long way from Wales of your own free will, and at your own expense. It is hardly necessary to add what an encouragement it was to those splendid boys.

" I am not in Sunderland now as often as I used to be, but every time I am, somebody says to me : ' Have you seen Jimmy lately ? ' They will never forget you. I should like them to have a book which records the events in the life of one of the greatest sportsmen I have had the honour to meet.

" Your sincere friend,

(Signed) CASTLEREAGH."

While on the subject of enthusiasm it would be well to mention two shining examples in Captain Horace and Mr. R. B. Alaway, respectively President and Honorary Secretary of the Middlesex Wanderers. They have been associated with that grand amateur football club for thirty-five years—since its inception —and the Club is an integral part of their lives.

They are planning, at the moment, the fiftieth Wanderers' tour abroad—I wonder if that is a record for any club ?

When I first met Horace and Bob Alaway I had no idea of the extent of their work for the Club, or for that matter for amateur sport in many ways. Too few people know of it, I feel, and I am happy to be associated with them. The Club was established primarily to raise first-class amateur teams for foreign tours, and they have done much to keep the level of British sport high in the minds of Continental sportsmen. Their horizons, too, are unlimited—I think they are waiting for the days of more general air travel to go further afield without interfering too much with the members' business lives.

I have had some good times playing with them, both at football and cricket. Incidentally I have umpired at a number of their cricket matches, not always with stern efficiency. I am fond of the game, but some of the rules will escape me at the vital moments! Most of their cricket is played abroad—they could tell you of keen cricketers in Germany, Belgium, Denmark, Holland, in fact most European countries.

The Wanderers, too, have done much for charity, and the establishment of the Richmond Boxing Day Regatta is surely unique. It has been running without a break for nearly twenty years, although its success was in considerable doubt at first. Boxing Day and wet-bobs hardly go together! They do at Richmond, however; girls as well as men turn out sometimes on piercing cold and murky days, the crowds along the towing path are always large, and the local hospitals and other charities benefit substantially.

There seems no limit to the versatility of the Club. The annual Sportsmen's Service at the Finsbury Town Hall is, of course, widely known. Fewer people know that it is connected with the Peel Institute, a Boys' Club which has a great influence on youngsters from the poorer London districts. The boys act as hosts for tea, after the service, and look forward to informal chats with prominent sportsmen, past and present, afterwards.

The Wanderers' Annual Dinner, too, is a remarkable function, because of the faithfulness of its members. One man, I'm told, comes from the Rhineland by air every year to dine with " his club." Every branch of sport is represented, and most nations. One might almost call it an informal Olympiad, with memories and reminiscences in place of new world records.

There was one trip to Leeds (I forget the date) for a charity when at the hotel Joe Beckett and Tommy Burns began to argue. The argument turned into a heated quarrel, and before anyone knew what was happening there were the two ex-champions bundling in at the bottom of the stairs ! The scrap did not last long, and most of us were too well-acquainted with the ring to be able to appreciate the free show. They laughed about it afterwards and remained good friends—I'm sure they'll forgive this reminder. Actually, quarrels between boxers are usually mild and of short life, and all spring from the keen enthusiasm a man must have if he is to get anywhere in the game.

In a way, these charity shows make a holiday, and good fun we usually get from them. That reminds me of my last trip to the States, in 1928, with no idea of trying to regain my lost crown. 'Lisbeth and I were anxious to see Frankie Burns—we never fail to correspond, and I shall never forget his help and that of his wife after the Pancho Villa disaster.

Frankie took me to the Elks' Club in Jersey City, I was made an honorary member, and amused the others by playing English snooker and billiards, very different from their all-cannon game. Among Frankie's many friends was Mayor Jimmy Walker, of New York fame.

Walker is a cheerful fellow, extremely friendly and likeable. He was with us when Frankie and I were talking about a ten days' holiday to Niagara Falls, and we were planning to hire a car.

" No, there's no need," said Walker, " I can lend you one."

After some argument, we accepted. The only blot on the trip to Niagara by road was the absence of Verdun, who had cut his foot badly. But David, 'Lisbeth and myself, as well as Frankie and his wife, thoroughly enjoyed the holiday.

Jimmy Walker is world-renowned, but I wonder how many people this side of the Atlantic can picture his jaunty figure, always immaculate and usually with a button-hole, his clothes never of a quiet shade, but green or mauve, with brilliant ties that must have been unrivalled. Men's clothing is more colourful in the States than in England, but " Mayor Jimmy " was a leader of the fashion.

It has been suggested that while I am writing I could with advantage give my opinion on the many boxers out of my weight, or who fought after my retirement. I'm not at all sure it would be of any benefit to anyone, although there are some who cannot be neglected. Carpentier, the man who brought a new fascination to the ring, is probably the most popular boxer to non-fighting people who has ever lived. He dispersed at long last the time-honoured and well-established idea that a professional boxer must be a rough and tough. And there was Dempsey, who was the finest heavy-weight of his era. I have always wished I had been able to stay in the States for the Dempsey-Carpentier fight, which the American won after a really good contest. To see Dempsey's defence against that prodigious straight right of Carpentier's must have been unique in boxing annals. Dempsey's little smile had a lot to recommend it. In quite a different way from his French contemporary, he had a great deal of charm,

although it did not appeal to so wide a " non-boxing "
public.

Only Jack Johnson, I think, was superior to
Dempsey in the heavy-weight class, which leads me
to an aside about negro boxers. Are they, as some
folk believe, superior to whites ? In my opinion a
black boxer will beat a white who has equal strength
and skill, but there are more *good* whites than negroes.
Coloured boxers are, admittedly, harder to teach and
to train, but once they have learned the technique
they never forget it. Their weakness is their stomach
and their strength in their jaw-bone, but it is surprising how many white boxers forget this when
fighting a man of colour.

Teach a negro to defend his stomach, however,
and he is practically unbeatable. (I'm talking about
champions, not chopping-blocks, of course.) Joe
Louis, to-day, reigns supreme among the heavy-
weights ; a fine boxer but not, I believe, as good as
Dempsey. But the most remarkable figure in modern
boxing is Henry Armstrong, now the world's welter,
light and feather-weight champion. This American
negro is the first man ever to hold three titles at
different weights—and probably he will be the last.
I have never seen him in action, but it is obvious
from the reports that he has the little touch of genius
that makes a good boxer into a world-beater of the
type who can give away as much as two stone and
win almost at leisure.

Two of the most unusual boxers for many years
were both in the heavy-weight class. It is almost a
crime to mention Primo Carnera and Gene Tunney in
the same breath, but in their differing ways they were

both oddities. (Gene may not agree !) I met Tunney
when he was with the Allied Services in this country,
and no man less like a professional heavy-weight has
come my way. Quiet, reserved, intellectual, he
carved a special niche for himself in boxing history.

So, also, did Carnera. He was more of a subject for
joking in fighting circles than a serious boxer, and in
the ring he had no control over his great size and
abnormal strength. I have heard it claimed that he
dare not hit too hard. Frankly, I don't believe it.
He could not, excepting by accident. Hitting in the
ring is a science that is not connected with physical
strength half as much as is made out. Timing (or
control) is the vital factor. Primo Carnera, amiable
fellow though he was, had no idea of directing or
timing his punches, and still less of making any
defensive play. His strength and stamina kept him
going where many others would have been knocked
out.

What of our other heavy-weights, or light-heavies ?

Len Harvey is one of the most scientific and I
think that if he fought as well as he boxed he would
be a world-beater. In this respect he has something
in common with Joe Beckett. But I have wondered
whether Len does not deliberately box, saving himself
from heavy punishment, in order to prolong his
career. There would be a lot to be said for that
attitude, although let me confess it as guesswork.

The Petersen-Harvey fights have had a great deal
of publicity. I mean no offence to Jack when I say
I think he has been lucky, because he came at a time
when there was a serious dearth of heavy-weights. He
is different from Harvey, being a fighter without Len's

boxing skill. But there is little doubt that they are well-matched boxers.

I think Jack Bloomfield would have gone further than he did but for the injury in his fight with Tom Gibbons. He had a really good straight left. But, as I have said before, he is flourishing nicely at his hotel and I hope he won't object to my saying I think he has proved one of the very few boxers who have had the good sense to save hard while earning money in the ring.

Kid Berg was a fine fighter—if only he had a little extra in his punches ! Peter Kane is another good boy just missing greatness. And there are countless others, who help to keep boxing on its high level as a world sport.

On the whole, however, it is safe to say that, since the Dempsey-Tunney-Carpentier era, there have been very few outstanding boxers : perhaps I should say boxers-cum-fighters. But there have been many exciting contests, and there still are many promising youngsters at the ring. Perhaps—I advance this as the vaguest theory—the change from small-money fights to big-money ones has made a difference. There is far more to fight for, these days, yet money is earned much more easily.

I remember broadcasting on the night of the Small Montana-Benny Lynch fight, at Wembley. I was rather disappointed with the show they put up, for there was a great deal of missing and little punching. On the other hand, I have missed deliberately myself a great deal. Let he who casts the first stone——

I have sometimes wondered whether Max Baer takes his fighting as seriously as he should. That astonishing

fight with Farr will live long in the memory of those
who saw it. Farr won, I thought deservingly, but
I had hoped he would go further than he has. There
is still plenty of time for him. In the days when I was
match-maker at Wimbledon (not so long ago, for I
first started back in the boxing world as a match-
maker) I made Farr's first London fight, with a
Frenchman whose name escapes me. I had hopes, too,
of managing Farr, but the arrangements fell through.
I still have hopes, now that I have the necessary
certificate from the Boxing Board of Control, to
manage some good big 'uns, and some good little
'uns. At the moment I am training at Wembley,
and my enthusiasm for boxing is, if possible, increasing.

Since the death of Jim Driscoll I have been reporting
for the *News of the World*. The advantages of it, in
my particular case, are manifold. The familiar
atmosphere of the ring does a lot to dismiss the
vagueness in my mind of old-time fights. I meet
boxers I had almost forgotten and grand hours pass
in comparing notes, remembering this punch and
that. And so I can keep well up to the minute with
the greatest of sports. Max Schmeling—a rather better
man, I think, than most people give him credit for—
was easily the winner in his recent Hamburg bout with
Ben Foord : but Ben is as courageous a battler as
I have seen.

So they go on, names without number.

It is difficult sometimes to know which makes the
greater impression, the genuine patron or the fighter
himself. Dempsey, Carpentier and others leave
unforgettable memories of their great days, but equally
unforgettable are the patrons of the quality of Sir

Harry Preston, Lord Lonsdale, Lord Derby, Jimmy White, and countless others.

But it is unwise, perhaps, to mention some and not others. Those who have played their various parts, in and out of the ring, will know well enough how much their efforts have been and are appreciated. It is surprising, too, how varied are the people interested in boxing. Steve Donoghue and Gordon Richards, once in the same stables, are keen fans. I remember looking at a four stone shrimp of a lad named Richards when I went to Jimmy White's stables and saying laughingly :

" Do you think you can ride winners ? "

" And why shouldn't I ? "

" Why, you're no horseman, surely."

" And you were once no boxer, but you are now : and I'm going to be a champion jockey ! "

Gordon has proved it. We frequently meet at dinners and talk over that early meeting. " Our Steve " by the way, would give his heart away, I think, if a man needed it ; or persuaded Steve he needed it.

I have met a host of people with boxing ambitions at one time or other in their lives. Only the other day I was talking with Mr. Michael Joseph, my publisher, who hardly looks old enough to remember much about my fighting days, although he tells me he has a son of eighteen.

" Not remember you ? " he laughed. " I was one of the little boys who used to gaze at you goggle-eyed, Jimmy. I even tried to emulate you at one time."

It was just after this that I fell into conversation with

an author with, apparently, a passion for figures, and he asked me the one question which left me standing. It was about boxing, too.

" How fast does a punch travel, Jimmy. Do you know ? "

" How—what ? "

" Fast. What speed does it go ? Faster than an express train, yes, but—as fast as a bullet, say ? "

" I don't see how you can tell," I said. " It's pretty fast, but it doesn't have to travel far. In fact it's hardly started before it arrives."

" Could you tie a piece of string on your thumb and have it connected with an instrument to measure speed?"

I chuckled.

" You could, but you'd look funny with a piece of string in your hand and a man anxious to knock a hole through you close by."

" I mean," he said with dignity, " in training."

Well, it may be possible, and if anyone has estimated the speed of punches, I should like to hear about it very much. But I don't think training punches go as fast as those when serious business is on foot. And somehow I don't think we shall ever see reports on these lines :

> " At the N.S.C., on Monday night, Bill Smith knocked out Jack Brown with an upper-cut to the chin travelling at a speed of 213.15 miles per hour. The average speed of punches during the fight was——"

But that is getting fantastic, perhaps.[1]

[1] Attempts have since been made to estimate the speed of punches, and so far it has been estimated at between 30 and 40 miles per hour.

I wonder, though. Many seemingly fantastic things have happened and are generally accepted now, particularly since my earliest fighting days. However absurd it seems, I once figured as the star in a film— one of the old, creaking silents, made before the War, and called " From Pit-boy to World's Champion." I remember having to quarrel bitterly with Tommy Noble during the film and also that I owned a lot of whippets (as the actor) so that Tommy and I could compete on the whippet track as well as in the ring. I would like to see that old film again, but I expect it has long since been destroyed.

It has not been my fortune to meet many film stars. I remember George Bancroft coming down to Cardiff ; a big, hearty man with a voice that was disappointingly tenor and not bass in real life although he could control it well. He was otherwise much the same as he appears on the screen.

Things forgotten, I said, and most of the things in this chapter do come under that heading, out of their right place in the story. But there is one thing I have never forgotten, and never shall. I have kept it deliberately until the last.

It was in May, 1930. The then Prince of Wales came to Cardiff Arms Park to attend a Welfare demonstration and I was one of the large crowd there. As he was walking round he caught sight of me and without hesitation broke the ranks. My mind flashed back to the various occasions when I had met him before, as he stretched out his hand.

" Hallo, Jimmy, it's a long time since we've met. How are you ? "

" I'm first class, thanks."

" That's good, but you're putting on weight," he smiled. " Where can we have a chat, I wonder ? "

An official remarked that the canteen was empty, and the Prince led the way there, chatting over old times, old fights, old memories. I think he was reluctant to go back to formal duties. I know it was a perfect example of his endearing habit of doing the last thing expected of him.

And so . . .

AFTERWORD

It's a long stretch of time from the 1938 publication date of Jimmy Wilde's book to the time, as I wrote in the foreword, when I came to know him in the latter half of the 'fifties. Another long stretch before he was admitted to Tegfan Ward of Whitchurch Hospital, Cardiff, in 1965.

As I was not yet born – in fact, it was the year in which my late parents married – when 'The Mighty Atom' fought his last fight, my eye-witness experience of seeing him in action comes only through highlights of a few of his major bouts on old 8mm film. But figures and tradition speak for themselves; a calculated record of 864 battles from dingy pit rooms, through fairground booths and little smoky fight halls to the great arenas. And he only lost four times in a career which, in truth, began before he was so much as into his 'teens.

Who can conceive a man with these statistics intimidating the minds of experienced, much bigger fighters? Wilde's reach was 66 inches, chest 31½ inches, waist 25¾ inches, thigh 21 inches, wrist 6¼ inches and biceps 11½ inches. Quite often he would weigh-in fully clothed to make 6 stone 12, and in America he also carried weights in his pockets besides wearing a hat because some States outlawed matches involving a big weight difference between the contestants.

But this is an afterword, and, as Jimmy makes clear in his story, his memory was never the same after the cruel beating he suffered at the hands of Pancho Villa. Another little-known truth is that Wilde never properly got over a horrifying car crash at Cadoxton, Glamorgan, in the early 'sixties. Add to that the fact that he was badly beaten-up by teenage thugs on a lonely Welsh railway station when on his way home after a charity function appearance . . . butted in the face and kicked by creatures unfit to have washed his jock-strap in the good days.

Wilde was a patient in Whitchurch Hospital for four years. The elderly were housed there mostly through suffering from senility. But Jimmy was diabetic as well and his memory had completely gone. In the early days he was not bed-ridden, though his clear blue eyes were somewhat vacant and he seemed to wear a permanent smile.

In 1968 he became bed-ridden and he never came to realise that his dear wife, Elizabeth, had died nearly two years earlier. Happily, the hospital nurses loved him and one of them, young enough to have been his grandchild, said that he looked more like an innocent young child rather than a once-great professional pugilist as the end drew nigh.

The Great Referee in the Sky finally counted Jimmy Wilde out aged seventy-six on 10 March 1969. He was quietly laid to rest in Barry four days later.